The PSYCHOTHERAPIES
of MARITAL DISHARMONY

The PSYCHOTHERAPIES

of MARITAL DISHARMONY

EDITED BY Bernard L. Greene, M.D.

THE FREE PRESS, *New York*

COLLIER-MACMILLAN LIMITED, *London*

For information, address:

THE FREE PRESS

A DIVISION OF THE MACMILLAN COMPANY

60 Fifth Avenue, New York, N.Y. 10011

Collier-Macmillan Canada, Ltd., Toronto, Ontario

DESIGNED BY SIDNEY SOLOMON

Library of Congress Catalog Card Number: 65-11320

TO *Franz Alexander,* WHO PERSONIFIED THE SPIRIT
OF EXPERIMENTATION IN PSYCHOTHERAPY

PREFACE

Each chapter in this book was originally presented in condensed form at the panel, "The Psychotherapies of Marital Disharmony," on March 20, 1964, in Chicago, Illinois, at the annual meeting of the American Orthopsychiatric Association. The Board of Directors of this organization has given permission to use the proceedings of the panel as a basis for this book.

In suggesting a panel on the psychotherapies of marital disharmony to the program committee of the American Orthopsychiatric Association, I was guided by the wish to achieve systematization—a theoretical utilization of each operational approach for maximum therapeutic effect—and not simply treatment by expediency. There is need for a study, conducted over a long period of time,* to determine the criteria for the various therapeutic methods to be presented by our contributors.

Bernard L. Greene, M.D.

*A tentative beginning in this direction was attempted in a paper presented at the annual meeting of the American Psychiatric Association in Los Angeles, May 7, 1964 (Bernard L. Greene and Noel Lustig, "Multi-Operational Psychotherapies of Marital Disharmony"). See also Reuben Hill, "A Critique of Contemporary Marriage and Family Research," *Social Forces*, 33 (March, 1955), 268; Jay Haley, "Marriage Therapy," *Archives of General Psychiatry*, 8 (1963), 213; Martin Grotjahn, "*Analytic* Family Therapy: A Survey of Trends in Research and Practice," Jules H. Masserman, ed., *Science and Psychoanalysis, II: Individual and Familial Dynamics* (New York: Grune & Stratton, Inc., 1958), 90-104; and John A. MacLeod, "Some Criteria for the Modification of Treatment Arrangements," Howard J. Parad and Roger R. Miller, eds., *Ego-Oriented Casework: Problems and Perspectives* (New York: Family Service Association of America, 1963), pp. 165-76.

CONTRIBUTORS

Nathan W. Ackerman, M.D.
Clinical Professor of Psychiatry, Columbia University;
Director of Professional Program, The Family Institute
(New York)

Betty P. Broadhurst, M.S.S.
Associate Professor of Social Work, The Graduate School
of Social Work, University of Denver, Denver, Colorado

Peter L. Giovacchini, M.D.
Clinical Professor of Psychiatry, College of Medicine,
University of Illinois; Clinical Associate, Chicago Insti-
tute for Psychoanalysis

Hilda M. Goodwin, D.S.W.
Assistant Professor of Family Study in Psychiatry, University of Pennsylvania

Bernard L. Greene, M.D.
Assistant Clinical Professor of Psychiatry, College of
Medicine, University of Illinois; Chief of the Marital
Department, Forest Hospital, Des Plaines, Illinois

Martin Grotjahn, M.D.
Clinical Professor of Psychiatry, University of Southern
California; Training Psychoanalyst, Southern California
Psychoanalytic Institute

Noel Lustig, M.D., Captain U.S.M.C.
Chief of Psychiatric Service, Madigan General Hospital,
Tacoma, Washington

Peter A. Martin, M.D.
Associate Clinical Professor of Psychiatry, Wayne State University College of Medicine

Emily H. Mudd, M.S.W., PH.D.
Professor of Family Study in Psychiatry, University of Pennsylvania

Otto Pollak, PH.D.
Professor of Sociology, University of Pennsylvania

Virginia M. Satir, A.C.S.W.
Director of Training, Family Project, Mental Research Institute, Palo Alto, California

Alfred P. Solomon, M.D.
Associate Clinical Professor of Psychiatry, College of Medicine, University of Illinois; Attending Psychiatrist, Presbyterian-St. Luke's Hospital, Chicago, Illinois

CONTENTS

The PSYCHOTHERAPIES
of MARITAL DISHARMONY

1

INTRODUCTION:
A MULTI-OPERATIONAL APPROACH
TO MARITAL PROBLEMS

Bernard L. Greene

Psychotherapy[1] is replete with rigidly held but widely varied doctrines. It is not unusual for experienced therapists to have difficulty in understanding and communicating in meaningful ways with colleagues trained in different schools. This difficulty has led to a state of relative isolation among therapists, which has too often prevented critical self-analysis and inhibited the exchange of ideas. Progress in other disciplines may go unnoted or be poorly understood or simply disparaged. We should pay heed to the wise words of Franz Alexander in his book, *The Scope of Psychoanalysis:* "Instead of progressive improvements of knowledge and practice, the tendency to rest on the laurels of the past appears in the form of dogmatism . . . . re-evaluation [of knowledge] necessarily leads to changes and requires constant revision of techniques of treatment and steady experimentation."[2] Differences exist among therapists in terms of knowledge, skill, personal aptitudes, and experience. Psychotherapies differ only in methods for achieving the same goals.

It is hoped that the contributors, who represent different theoretical systems with their various theories and constructs, will feed material to other workers, will promote disciplined impartiality, will stimulate our imaginations, and will challenge our biases in regard to psychotherapy. Most therapists are so intimidated by the complexity of marital conflicts that they hold dogmatically to one theory or another, while refusing to look at the work of those who think differently.[3] As we select and utilize available knowledge, we shall begin to integrate new systems and to enlarge our therapeutic scope. Actually, most teachers, instead of comparing and pointing out different approaches, present one technique or another as the primary method, the "good" one, while other methods are merely tolerated or very often even disparaged.[4]

The complexity of our society[5] results in great variation in marital patterns.[6] This variation necessitates greater flexibility in therapeutic techniques. Clinical necessity, therapeutic failures, advancing knowledge,[7] and the changing sociocultural scene[8] necessitate further flexibility in technique. The therapist must evaluate the problem of each couple and must transcend his personal preferences in order to apply what is most beneficial in a given conflicted marriage. The therapist must decide intuitively, from couple

Table 1—Couples Observed in the Past Ten Years

Year	Rejects-refusals	Counseling	Concurrent	Conjoint	Combined	Collaborative	Classical analysis
1954*	0	0	0	0	0	3	1
1955	3	4	3	0	0	4	1
1956	1	4	3	0	0	4	1
1957	1	3	3	0	0	2	2
1958	1	2	8	0	0	2	6
1959	2	4	12	0	0	1	6
1960	5	4	17	0	0	1	3
1961	5	4	17	0	0	0	3
1962	6	10	12	3	2	1	2
1963	8	12	16	7	10	4	4
1964*	12	18	12	14	14	4	5
Totals	44	54**	49**	18**	19**	15**	20**

Total Couples: 219

*Figures given are for six-month periods only.
**The totals do not represent addition of figures in each column but are cumulative, as therapy may overlap from one year to another.

to couple, which technique or combination of techniques is most applicable at any particular moment. He must be able to tailor his approach to the couple's individual, as well as mutual, needs.

This book is organized from a practical point of view. From personal experience[9] with *all* the operational approaches to be discussed in this book (see Table 1), from personal conversations and communications, and from culling the literature (see Bibliography, pp. 9-14), I have proposed a "six C" classification of techniques. At the present time, the various techniques consist of

I. *Supportive therapy*
  A. Counseling—an orientation stressing sociocultural forces and explicitly acknowledging the implications of the "here and now" situation.
II. *Intensive therapy*
  A. Classical psychoanalysis—an individually oriented approach.
  B. Collaborative—the marital partners are treated by different therapists, who communicate for the purpose of maintaining the marriage.
  C. Concurrent—both spouses are treated individually but synchronously by the same therapist.
  D. Conjoint—both partners are seen together in the same session by the same therapist.
  E. Combined—a combination of
    1. individual, concurrent, and conjoint sessions in various purposeful combinations;
    2. analytic family therapy; and
    3. group psychotherapy.[10]

In the evolution of our methodology of therapy, we began by focusing upon the individual, on the *dyadic,* one-to one relationship. We explored the patient's environment only to the extent necessary for achieving our therapeutic aim of intrapsychic structural changes. Treatment failures in some cases necessitated focal shifts to include the relationship between husband and wife, as well as their individual personalities. The *triadic* approaches, including concurrent, conjoint, and combined techniques, were thus developed. Finally, because of therapeutic impasses with certain couples, we had to move beyond the two person relationship to include children who were contributing to marital disharmony. Our modes of treatment can thus be visualized, *in terms of a spectrum of therapeutic settings,* with the dyadic approaches of classical and collaborative techniques at one end; the triadic approaches of concurrent, conjoint, and combined analytic therapies in the middle; and analytic family therapy at the other end. The spectrum concept is not meant to establish a dogmatic therapeutic hierarchy but rather to offer a guide to the available techniques for helping couples and to clarify the psychotherapeutic resources available. Furthermore, this spectrum concept does not imply that any one therapist can be or is even expected to be talented or interested in all the varied techniques. But it is expected that the couple's needs be given prime consideration and, furthermore, that the therapist be prepared to identify the optimum mode of therapy, even though he himself cannot continue with that form of treatment.

If we look for complications in our various approaches, we shall certainly find them in our accustomed theoretical constructs (see Dr. Giovacchini's critique in Chapter 4). If we are orthodox, we can raise many objections—for example, the individual loses the therapeutic advantages of being the primary concern of the therapist's attention, the patient is reluctant to voice certain of his feelings in the presence of his partner for fear of later retaliation, and so forth. In a measure, these and other considerations and points are valid. Such objections, however, instead of detracting from the value of the marital approaches we have outlined, should enhance our understanding of marital dynamics. They make possible a shift from viewing the psychopathology of the individual as the central problem to seeing it as a symptom contributing to a disturbed marriage. They represent a direct approach to the marital unit as a whole.

As we learn to use all available knowledge, we shall find our points of view broadened, our skills sharpened, and our ability to meet the needs of the many couples with conflicted marriages increased. The clinical contributions in this book, taken together, describe the nascent operational approaches for treating marital disharmony. It is for future experimentation and investigation to develop them further and more systematically. Such development will, we hope, conform to the accepted scientific principles of prediction, design, control, and quantification.

NOTES

1. Alex H. Kaplan, in "Social Work Therapy and Psychiatric Psychotherapy," *Archives of General Psychiatry,* 9 (November, 1963), 95, gives a good definition of psychotherapy, "as a psychological treatment whereby a trained therapist develops a planned relationship with a patient or client with the expressed purpose of relieving suffering, it will include therapy carried out by a variety of individuals with differing backgrounds and training."

2. Franz Alexander, *The Scope of Psychoanalysis* (New York: Basic Books, Inc., 1961), pp. 541-4.

3. W. W. Meissner, in an excellent comprehensive survey of the literature on the family, has pinpointed the "issues and problems which must be thought through in working toward an understanding of the family." See "Thinking About the Family—Psychiatric Aspects," *Family Process,* 3 (March, 1964), 1-40. Gregory Bateson, Don D. Jackson, Jay Haley, and John Weakland describe the "double bind" situation in "'Toward a Theory of Schizophrenia," *Behavioral Science,* 1 (October, 1956), 251-64. See also Edward J. Carroll and Aldo W. Mell, "An Assessment of Family Interviewing," paper presented at the panel, "Family Interaction Tests," at the annual meeting of the American Orthopsychiatric Association, Chicago, Illinois, March 20, 1964; Robert J. Drechsler and Marvin I. Shapiro, "A Procedure for Direct Observation of Family Interaction in a Child Guidance Clinic," *Psychiatry,* 24 (May, 1961), 163-70; Antonio J. Ferreira, "Family Myth and Homeostasis," *Archives of General Psychiatry,* 9 (November, 1963), 457-63; Jackson, Jules Riskin, and Virginia M. Satir, "A Method of Analysis of a Family Interview," *Archives of General Psychiatry,* 5 (1961), 321-39; Jan Ehrenwald, *Neurosis in the Family and Patterns of Psychosocial Defense* (Hoeber ed.; New York: Harper & Row, Publishers, 1963); Irene M. Josselyn, "The Family as a Psychological Unit," *Social Casework,* 34 (1953), 336-43; Cora Kasius, *Social Casework in the Fifties: Selected Articles, 1951-1960* (New York: Family Service Association of America, 1962); Florence R. Kluckhohn and John P. Spiegel, *Integration and Conflict in Family Behavior* (Report No. 27 [Topeka, Kansas: Group for the Advancement of Psychiatry, 1954]); Nestor C. Kohut, *A Manual on Marital Reconciliations* (Chicago: Adams Press, 1964); Gardner Murphy, "New Knowledge about Family Dynamics," *Social Casework,* 40 (1959), 363-70; Herbert A. Otto, "The Family Resource Development Program: The Production of Criteria for Assessing Family Strength," paper presented at the National Con-

ference on Social Welfare, New York City, May, 1962; Howard J. Parad and Roger R. Miller, eds., *Ego-Oriented Casework: Problems and Perspectives* (New York: Family Service Association of America, 1963); Harold Sampson, Sheldon L. Messinger, Robert D. Towne, David Ross, Florine Livson, Mary-Dee Bowers, Lester Cohen, and Kate S. Dorst, "The Mental Hospital and Marital Family Ties," *Social Problems,* 9 (1961), 141-55; Spiegel, "Homeostatic Mechanisms Within the Family," Iago Galdston, ed., *The Family in Contemporary Society* (New York: International Universities Press, Inc., 1958), pp. 73-89; Fred L. Strodtbeck, "Husband-Wife Interaction Over Revealed Differences," *American Sociological Review,* 16 (1951), 468-73; Strodtbeck, "Instruments Used in the Study of Family Interaction by the Revealed Difference Method," Social Psychology Laboratory, University of Chicago, November 6, 1962; James L. Tichener, Thomas D'Zmura, Myra Golden, and Richard Emerson, "Family Transaction and Derivation of Individuality," *Family Process,* 2 (March, 1963), 95-120; Walter Toman, *Family Constellation* (New York: Springer Publishing Co., Inc., 1961); Francis J. Turner, "A Comparison of Procedures in the Treatment of Clients with Two Different Value Orientations," *Social Casework,* 45 (May, 1964), 273-7; Ferdinand van der Veen, "The Family-Concept Q-Sort," Greater Kansas City Mental Health Foundation, Kansas City, Missouri; Van der Veen, B. Huebner, Barbara Jorgens, and P. Neja, "Relationships Between the Parents Concept of the Family and Family Adjustment," *American Journal of Orthopsychiatry,* 34 (January, 1964), 45-55; and Alice L. Voiland and Associates, *Family Casework Diagnosis* (New York: Columbia University Press, 1962). In the current literature, more attention is being paid to the sudden acceleration of personality maturation in response to an important life crisis or the psychopathological sequences that often begin or are aggravated at such times—the so-called "crisis" studies. One of the earliest crisis studies was that of Erich Lindemann, "Symptomatology and Management of Acute Grief," *American Journal of Psychiatry,* 101 (September, 1944), 141-8. See also Gerald Caplan, "Patterns of Parents Response to the Crisis of Premature Birth," *Psychiatry,* 23 (November, 1960), 365-74; Rhona Rapoport, "Normal Crises, Family Structure and Mental Health," *Family Process,* 2 (March, 1963), 68-80; Harold L. Rausch, Wells Goodrich, and John D. Campbell, "Adaptation to the First Years of Marriage," *Psychiatry,* 26 (November, 1963), 368-80; and Paul Glasser, who, in "Changes in Family Equilibrium During Psychotherapy," *Family Process,* 2 (September, 1963), 245-64, has provided an excellent bibliography on family crisis studies, marital adjustment studies, family development theory, role theory, and social psychiatry.

4. Leon Yochelson, in a recent academic lecture, decried the complacent attitude toward sectarianism in psychiatry that "has created a significant problem for the teacher who has not found the single

treatment which, like a '606,' could be expected to apply cure to all instances of psychological disorder." He suggests that training programs be geared "to devote greater attention to the teaching of indications for each of the several treatment possibilities available to the psychiatrist." See "Sectarianism in Psychiatry," *American Journal of Psychiatry*, 120 (June, 1964), 1143-8.

5. The following sources are useful in understanding the complexity of our society: Nathan W. Ackerman, *The Psychodynamics of Family Life* (New York: Basic Books, Inc., 1958), which presents a way of understanding health through the emotional give and take of family relationships and outlines a conceptual approach to emotional disturbance in the individual through analysis of the psychological content of his family experience; Ackerman, Frances L. Beatman, and Sanford N. Sherman, *Exploring the Base for Family Therapy* (New York: Family Service Association of America, 1961), which furnishes a group of succinctly organized papers constituting an important addition to the literature on the family; Robert O. Blood, Jr., *Marriage* (New York: The Free Press of Glencoe, 1962), a useful synthesis of the scientific literature on marriage, in which the concept of personal relationships is the central theme; Theodore Lidz and Stephen Fleck, "Schizophrenia, Human Integration and the Role of the Family," Jackson, ed., *Etiology of Schizophrenia* (New York: Basic Books, Inc., 1959), pp. 323-45; and Roland G. Tharp, "Psychological Patterning in Marriage," *Psychological Bulletin*, 60 (March, 1963), 1-24, an excellent article in which theory and research are reviewed and integrated with sociological data on mate selection and marital happiness, including an extensive bibliography.

6. See Edmund Bergler, *Unhappy Marriage and Divorce* (New York: International Universities Press, Inc., 1946), pp. 99-150; Murray Bowen, "The Origin and Development of Schizophrenia in the Family," paper read at Forest Hospital, Des Plaines, Illinois, May 24, 1961; Norbert Bromberg, "On Polygamous Women," paper presented at the annual meeting of the American Psychoanalytic Association, Atlantic City, May, 1960; John R. Cavanagh, "The Durable Incompatible Marriage: Psychological Characteristics of the Mates," *Southern Medical Journal*, 55 (April, 1962), 396-400; E. J. Cleveland and W. D. Longaker, "Neurotic Patterns in the Family," A. H. Leighton, J. H. Clausen, and R. N. Wilson, eds., *Explorations in Social Psychiatry* (New York: Basic Books, Inc., 1957), pp. 167-200; Marc H. Hollender, "Marriage and Divorce," *Archives of General Psychiatry*, 1 (December, 1959), 657-61; Lidz, Alice R. Cornelison, Fleck, and Dorothy Terry, "The Intrafamilial Environment of Schizophrenic Patients: II. Marital Schism and Marital Skew," *American Journal of Psychiatry*, 114 (September, 1957), 241-8; Lidz, Beulah Parker, and Cornelison, "The Role of the Father in the Family Environment of the Schizophrenic Patient," *American Journal of Psychiatry*, 113 (August, 1956),

126-32; Howard E. Mitchell, "Application of the Kaiser Method to Marital Pairs," *Family Process,* 2 (1963), 265-79; Riskin, "Methodology for Studying Family Interaction," *Archives of General Psychiatry,* 8 (April, 1963), 343-8; G. J. Sarwer-Foner, "Patterns of Marital Relationship," *American Journal of Psychotherapy,* 17 (January, 1963), 31-44; Alberto C. Serrano, Eugene C. McDonald, Harold A. Goolishian, Robert MacGregor, and Agnes M. Ritchie, "Adolescent Maladjustment and Family Dynamics," *American Journal of Psychiatry,* 118 (April, 1962), 897-901; and Lyman C. Wynne, Irving M. Ryckoff, Juliana Day, and Stanley I. Hirsch, "Pseudo-Mutuality in the Family Relations of Schizophrenics," *Psychiatry,* 21 (May, 1958), 205-20.

7. H. V. Dicks, "Object Relations Theory and the Marital Studies," *British Journal of Medical Psychology,* 36 (1963), 125-9, comments in Chapter 6, note 12 (p. 119); and Eric Berne, *Transactional Analysis in Psychotherapy* (New York: Grove Press, 1961), pp. 211-23.

8. The rapid and extensive structural changes that have influenced the patterning of American families have been the object of considerable study by social scientists. A thought-provoking book by Talcott Parsons and Robert F. Bales, *Family, Socialization and Interaction Process* (New York: The Free Press of Glencoe, 1960), explores the intimate interrelationships of sociology, anthropology, and psychology. Another excellent book, which organizes a wide variety of family phenomena, is by Norman W. Bell and Ezra F. Vogel, eds., *A Modern Introduction to the Family* (New York: The Free Press of Glencoe, 1960). See also Hill, "The Changing American Family," *Social Welfare Forum* (New York: Columbia University Press, 1957); Phillip Fellin and Eugene Litwak: "Neighborhood Cohesion Under Conditions of Mobility," *American Sociological Review,* 28 (June, 1963), 364; Leon Eisenberg, "The Family in the Mid-Twentieth Century, *Social Welfare Forum* (New York: Columbia University Press, 1960), p. 98; Robert F. Winch and Robert McGinnis, eds., *Selected Studies in Marriage and the Family* (New York: Holt, Rinehart & Winston, Inc., 1953); M. F. Ashley Montagu, "Marriage—A Cultural Perspective," V. W. Eisenstein, ed., *Neurotic Interaction in Marriage* (New York: Basic Books, Inc., 1956), pp. 3-9; Galdston, ed., *The Family in Contemporary Society* (New York: International Universities Press, Inc., 1958); Harold T. Christensen and George C. Carpenter, "Timing Patterns in the Development of Sexual Intimacy: An Attitudinal Report on Three Modern Western Societies," *Marriage and Family Living,* 24 (February, 1962), 30-5; Winston Ehrman, *Premarital Dating Behavior* (New York: Holt, Rinehart & Winston, Inc., 1959); Robert D. Hess and Gerald Handel, *Family Worlds* (Chicago: University of Chicago Press, 1963); James H. S. Bossard and Eleanor S. Boll, *Why Marriages Go Wrong* (New York: The Ronald Press Company, 1958); Frances Lomas Feldman, *The Family in a Money World* (New York: Family Service Association of America, 1961); J. C. Flugel, *The Psy-*

choanalytic Study of the Family (London: Hogarth Press, 1948); and Morton Levitt and Ben Rubenstein, "Some Observations on the Relationship Between Cultural Variants and Emotional Disorders," which presents a stimulating survey of the problems of modern living and resulting identities and alienation of individuals, in *American Journal of Orthopsychiatry,* 34 (April, 1964), 423-32.

9. The editor and his colleagues are engaged in an on-going therapeutic-action research program, now in its ninth year, for couples undergoing marital discord. The first article, published in 1959, was a description of our theoretical thinking and therapeutic technique as they were at that time. See Bernard L. Greene, "Marital Disharmony: Concurrent Analysis of Husband and Wife. I. Preliminary Report," *Diseases of the Nervous System,* 21 (February, 1960), 1-6. Details of our project have been reported in other papers. See Alfred P. Solomon and Greene, "Marital Disharmony: Concurrent Therapy of Husband and Wife by the Same Psychiatrist. III. An Analysis of the Therapeutic Elements and Action," *Diseases of the Nervous System,* 24 (January, 1963), 1-8; Greene and Solomon, "Marital Disharmony: Concurrent Psychoanalytic Therapy of Husband and Wife by the Same Psychiatrist. IV. The Triangular Transference Transactions," *American Journal of Psychotherapy,* 17 (July, 1963), 443-56; and Greene, Solomon, and Noel Lustig, "The Psychotherapies of Marital Disharmony with Special Reference to Marriage Counseling," *Medical Times,* 9 (1963), 243-56.

10. This approach is not dealt with in this book, as there are a number of excellent papers and books on the subject. See Chapter 8, Note 6 (p. 150); and bibliography at end of Jack C. Westman, Donald J. Carek, and John F. McDermott, "A Comparison of Married Couples in the Same and Separate Therapy Groups," paper presented at the annual conference of the American Group Psychotherapy Association, New York City, January 24, 1964.

BIBLIOGRAPHY

Bardill, Donald R., and Joseph J. Bevilacqua. "Family Interviewing by Two Caseworkers," *Social Casework,* 45 (May, 1964), 278-82.

Beatman, Frances L. "Family Interaction: Its Significance for Diagnosis and Treatment," *Cora Kasius, ed., Social Casework in the Fifties.* New York: Family Service Association of America, 1962, pp. 212-25.

Bell, John E. *Family Group Therapy.* U. S. Dept. of Health, Education, and Welfare, Pub. Health Monograph 64.

Bell, Norman W. "Extended Family Relations of Disturbed and Well Families," *Family Process,* 1 (September, 1962), 175-93.

Bird, H. Waldo, and Peter A. Martin. "Countertransference in Psychotherapy of Marriage Partners," *Psychiatry,* 19 (1956), 353-60.

Bowen, Murray. "Family Psychotherapy," *American Journal of Orthopsychiatry,* 31 (1961), 40-60.

Carroll, Edward J. "Family Therapy—Some Observations and Comparisons," *Family Process,* 3 (March, 1964), 178-85.

————. "Treatment of the Family as a Unit," *Pennsylvania Medical Journal,* 63 (January, 1960), 57-62.

Carroll, Edward J., C. Glenn Cambor, Jay V. Leopold, Miles D. Miller, and Walter J. Reis. "Psychotherapy of Marital Couples," *Family Process,* 2 (March, 1963), 25-33.

Chance, Erika. *Families in Treatment.* New York: Basic Books, Inc., 1959.

Chope, H. D., and Lillian Blackford. "The Chronic Problem Family: San Mateo County's Experience," *American Journal of Orthopsychiatry,* 33 (April, 1963), 462-8.

Cornelison, Alice R. "Casework Interviewing as a Research Technique in a Study of Families of Schizophrenic Patients," *Mental Hygiene,* 44 (October, 1960), 551-9.

Curtis, James L., Melly Simon, Frances L. Boykin, and Emma R. Noe. "Observations on 29 Multiproblem Families," *American Journal of Orthopsychiatry,* 34 (April, 1964), 510-6.

Dreikurs, Rudolph. "Techniques and Dynamics of Multiple Psychotherapy," *Psychiatric Quarterly,* 24 (October, 1950), 788-99.

Elkin, Meyer. "Short-Contact Counseling in a Conciliation Court," *Social Casework,* 43 (April, 1962), 1-7.

Faucett, Emily C. "Multiple-Client Interviewing: A Means of Assessing Family Processes," *Social Casework,* 43 (1962), 114-20.

Flesch, Regina. "Treatment Goals and Techniques in Marital Discord," *Journal of Social Casework* (1949), pp. 382-8.

Friedman, Alfred S. "Family Therapy as Conducted in the Home," *Family Process,* 1 (March, 1962), 132-40.

Garret, Annette. *Interviewing—Its Principles and Methods.* New York: Family Service Association of America, 1962.

Geist, Joanne, and Norman M. Gerber. "Joint Interviewing: A Treatment Technique With Marital Partners," *Social Casework,* 41 (May, 1960), 76-83.

Gomberg, M. Robert. "Family-Oriented Treatment of Marital Problems," Cora Kasius, ed., *Social Casework in the Fifties.* New York: Family Service Association of America, 1962, pp. 198-212.

Goodwin, Hilda, and Emily H. Mudd. "Marriage Counseling," A. Ellis and A. Abarbanel, eds., *Encyclopedia of Sexual Behavior.* New York: Hawthorn Books, Inc., 1961, pp. 685-95.

Gralnick, Alexander. "Family Psychotherapy: General and Specific Considerations," *American Journal of Orthopsychiatry,* 32 (1962), 515-25.

Green, Richard. "Collaborative and Conjoint Therapy Combined," *Family Process,* 3 (March, 1964), 90-8.

Green, Sidney L. "Psychoanalytic Contributions to Casework Treatment of Marital Problems," *Social Casework,* 35 (December, 1954), 419-23.

Greenberg, Irwin M., Ira Glick, Sandra Match, and Sylvia S. Riback. "Family Therapy: Indications and Rationale," *Archives of General Psychiatry,* 10 (January, 1964), 7-24.

Grinker, Roy R., Sr., Helen MacGregor, Kate Selan, Annette Klein, and Janet Kohrman. *Psychiatric Social Work. A Transactional Case Book.* New York: Basic Books, Inc., 1961. This book is a superb work for the therapist who wishes to apply transactional concepts to psychotherapy.

Grotjahn, Martin. *Psychoanalysis and the Family Neurosis.* New York: W. W. Norton and Company, Inc., 1960. Must reading! The therapist will be well repaid for a careful reading of this most stimulating book.

Gullerud, Ernest N., and Virginia Lee Harlan. "Four-Way Joint Interviewing in Marital Counseling," *Social Casework,* 43 (December, 1962), 532-7.

Hallowitz, David, Robert G. Clement, and Albert V. Cutter. "The Treatment Process with Both Parents Together," *American Journal of Orthopsychiatry,* 27 (July, 1957), 587-601.

Hallowitz, David, and Albert V. Cutter. "Collaborative Diagnostic and Treatment Process with Parents," *Social Work,* 39 (July, 1958), pp. 90-6.

Handlon, Joseph H., and Morris B. Parloff. "The Treatment of Patient and Family as a Group: Is It Group Psychotherapy?" *International Journal of Group Psychotherapy,* 12 (1962), 132-41.

Herndon, C. Nash, and Ethel M. Nash. "Premarriage and Marriage Counseling," *Journal of the American Medical Association,* 180 (May, 1962), 395-401.

Hey, Richard N., and Emily H. Mudd. "Recurring Problems in Marriage Counseling," *Marriage and Family Living,* 21 (May, 1959), 127-9.

Hollis, Florence. *Casework—A Psychosocial Therapy.* New York: Random House, Inc., 1964.

Huneus, Eugenia. "A Dynamic Approach to Marital Problems," *Social Casework,* 44 (March, 1963), 142-8.

Jackson, Don D. "Family Interaction, Family Homeostasis and Some Implications for Conjoint Family Psychotherapy," Jules H. Masserman, ed., *Science and Psychoanalysis: II. Individual and Family Dynamics.* New York: Grune & Stratton, Inc., 1958, pp. 122-41.

Jackson, Don D., and John H. Weakland. "Conjoint Family Therapy," *Psychiatry,* 24 (1961), 30-45.

Jackson, James, and Martin Grotjahn. "The Concurrent Psychotherapy of a Latent Schizophrenic and His Wife," *Psychiatry,* 22 (May, 1959), 153-60.

Jolesch, Miriam. "Casework Treatment of Young Married Couples," *Social Casework,* 43 (May, 1962), 245-51.

Konopka, Gisela. "Group Work Techniques in Joint Interviewing," National Conference of Social Workers, *Social Welfare Forum.* New York: Columbia University Press, 1957.

Krich, Aaron. "A Reluctant Counselee: A Specimen Case," Emily H. Mudd and Aaron Krich, eds., *Man and Wife.* New York: W. W. Norton and Company, Inc., 1957, pp. 258-75.

Laidlaw, Robert L. "Marriage Counseling," Samuel Liebman, ed., *Understanding Your Patient.* Philadelphia: J. B. Lippincott Co., 1957, p. 132.

————. "The Psychotherapy of Marital Problems," *Progress in Psychotherapy,* Vol. V. New York: Grune & Stratton, Inc., 1960, pp. 140-7.

Leader, Arthur L. "The Role of Intervention in Family-Group Treatment," *Social Casework,* 45 (June, 1964), 327-32.

Lehrman, Nathaniel S. "The Joint Interview: An Aid to Psychotherapy and Family Stability," *American Journal of Psychotherapy,* 17 (1963), 83-93.

Liek, Robert K., and L. K. Northwood. "The Classification of Family Interaction Problems for Treatment Purposes," paper read at the National Council on Family Relations, August, 1963.

Lindberg, Dwaine R., and Anne W. Wosmek. "The Use of Family Sessions in Foster Home Care," *Social Casework,* 44 (March, 1963), 137-41.

MacGregor, Robert. "Multiple Impact Psychotherapy with Families," *Family Process,* 1 (March, 1962), 15-29.

Martin, Peter A., and H. Waldo Bird. "An Approach to the Psychotherapy of Marriage Partners," *Psychiatry,* 16 (1953), 123-7.

Minuchin, Salvador, Edgar Auerswald, Charles H. King, and Clara Rabinowitz: "The Study and Treatment of Families That Produce Multiple Acting-Out Boys," *American Journal of Orthopsychiatry,* 34 (January, 1964), 125-33.

Mittlemann, Bela. "Complimentary Neurotic Reactions in Intimate Relationships," *Psychoanalytic Quarterly,* 13 (1944), 479-91.

————. "The Concurrent Analysis of Married Couples," *Psychoanalytic Quarterly,* 17 (1948), 182.

Mudd, Emily H. *The Practice of Marriage Counseling.* New York: Association Press, 1951.

————. "Psychiatry and Marital Problems," *Eugenics Quarterly,* 2 (1955), 110-7.

Mudd, Emily H., and Martin Goldberg. "How to Help Your Patients with Marital Problems," Consultant S K & F Laboratories, 1961.

Oakey, Ruth C. "Meeting the Problems of Intake in Child Guidance and Marital Counseling," *Mental Hygiene,* 45 (January, 1961), 53-6.

Oberndorf, Clarence P. "Psychoanalysis of Married Couples," *Psychoanalytic Review,* 25 (1938), 453-75.

Parad, Howard J. "Brief Ego-Oriented Casework with Families in Crisis," Howard J. Parad and Roger R. Miller, eds., *Ego-Oriented Casework.* New York: Family Service Association of America, 1963, pp. 145-64.

Parloff, Morris B. "The Family in Psychotherapy," *Archives of General Psychiatry,* 45 (1961), 445-51.

Patterson, Jane E., and Florence E. Cyr. "The Use of the Home Visit in Present-day Social Work," *Social Casework,* 41 (1960), 184-91.

Peltz, William L. "Practical Aspects of Marriage Counseling," Emily H. Mudd and Aaron Krich, eds., *Man and Wife.* New York: W. W. Norton & Company, Inc., 1957, pp. 242-57.

Pollak, Otto, and Donald Brieland. "The Midwest Seminar on Family Diagnosis and Treatment," *Social Casework,* 42 (July, 1961), 319-24.

Regensburg, Jeannette. "Application of Psychoanalytic Concepts to Casework Treatment of Marital Problems," *Social Casework,* 35 (December, 1954), 424-32.

Reidy, Joseph J. "Family Treatment Approaches," *American Journal of Orthopsychiatry,* 32 (January, 1962), 133-42.

Richmond, Alvin H., and Agnes Lauga. "Some Observations Concerning the Role of Children in the Disruption of Family Homeostasis," *American Journal of Orthopsychiatry,* 33 (July, 1963), 757-9.

Rosenthal, Maurice J. "Collaborative Therapy with Parents at Child Guidance Clinics," *Social Casework* (January, 1954).

Sacks, Patricia. "Establishing the Diagnosis in Marital Problems," *Journal of Social Casework* (1948), 181-7.

Sager, Clifford J. "Concurrent Individual and Group Analytic Psychotherapy," *American Journal of Orthopsychiatry,* 30 (April, 1960), 225-41.

Saul, Leon J., Robert W. Laidlaw, Janet F. Nelson, Ralph Ormsby, Abraham Stone, Sidney Eisenberg, Kenneth E. Appel, and Emily H. Mudd. "Can One Partner Be Successfully Counseled Without the Other?" *Marriage and Family Living,* 15 (February, 1953), 61-4.

Scherz, Frances H. "Multiple-Client Interviewing: Treatment Implications," *Social Casework,* 43 (1962), 120-5.

Shapiro, David S., and Leonard T. Maholick. "A Systematic Approach to Mental Health Assessment and Counseling," *Mental Hygiene,* 46 (1962), 393-9.

Shellow, Robert S., Bertram S. Brown, and James W. Osberg. "Family Group Therapy in Retrospect: Four Years and Sixty Families," *Family Process,* 2 (March, 1963), 52-67.

Shereshefsky, Pauline M. "Family Unit Treatment in Child Guidance," *Social Work,* 8 (October, 1963), 4.

Sherman, Sanford N. "Joint Interviews in Casework Practice," *Social Work,* 4 (April, 1959), 20-8.

Sholtis, Helen S. "Management of Marriage Counseling Cases," *Social Casework,* 45 (February, 1964), 71-8.

Skidmore, Rex A. "The Joint Interview in Marriage Counseling," *Marriage and Family Living,* 17 (1955), 4.

Starr, Phillip H. "The 'Triangular' Treatment Approach in Child Therapy: Complementary Psychotherapy of Mother and Child," *American Journal of Psychotherapy,* 10 (1956), 40-53.

Thomas, Alexander. "Simultaneous Psychotherapy with Marital Partners," *American Journal of Psychotherapy,* 10 (October, 1956), 716-27.

Vesper, Sue. "Casework Aimed at Supporting Marital Role Reversal," *Social Casework,* 43 (June, 1962), 303-7.

Watson, Andrew S. "The Conjoint Psychotherapy of Marriage Partners," *American Journal of Orthopsychiatry,* 33 (November, 1963), 912-21.

Weisberg, Miriam. "Joint Interviewing with Marital Partners," *Social Casework,* 45 (April, 1964), 221-9.

Weiss, Viola W. "Multiple-Client Interviewing: An Aid in Diagnosis," *Social Casework,* 43 (March, 1962), 14.

Weiss, Viola W., and Russell R. Monroe. "A Framework for Understanding Family Dynamics," Cora Kasius, ed., *Social Casework in the Fifties.* New York: Family Service Association of America, 1962, pp. 175-98.

Whitaker, Carl A. "Psychotherapy with Couples," *American Journal of Psychotherapy,* 12 (January, 1958), 18-23.

Wynne, Lyman C. "The Study of Intrafamilial Alignments and Splits in Exploratory Family Therapy," Nathan W. Ackerman, Frances L. Beatman, and Sanford H. Sherman, eds., *Exploring the Base for Family Therapy.* New York: Family Service Association of America, 1961, pp. 95-115.

2

SOCIOLOGICAL AND PSYCHOANALYTIC CONCEPTS IN FAMILY DIAGNOSIS

Otto Pollak

We owe to Freud our understanding of the unconscious forces involved in marital disharmony. His conceptual model and therapeutic approach were, however, directed toward the individual. On the other hand, behavioral scientists have for a long time viewed society and the family as the sources of psychopathology in the individual. The time has passed when responsibility for marital disharmony and treatment must be placed exclusively on one spouse. The more realistic and current trend recognizes marital discord as a complex of interlocking transactions that cannot be divided into "internal" and "external" categories. Because marriage involves two people and is thus a miniature social system and because the partners' personalities play an important role in the outcome of a marriage, a theoretical frame of reference was sought that would combine these two areas. Fortunately, Professor Pollak has, with his characteristic clarity, given considerable thought to this problem and has written a challenging book entitled Integrating Sociological and Psychoanalytic Concepts.

In recent years the terms "family diagnosis" and "family therapy" have been widely used. Their coequal use, however, conceals a paradox. While family therapy has become a reality of practice, family diagnosis has remained a postulate. There are as yet no generally accepted typologies of marital or family disorders that would permit a precise classification on which a specific treatment plan could be based.[1] It is the purpose of this paper to make a start toward meeting this demand by an attempt to use sociological and psychoanalytic concepts to characterize various forms of marital relationship. This characterization will suggest types of dysfunction between the marriage partners and their possible causation in terms of secondary gains in the realm of psychodynamics and of unresolved problems created by social change.

In an attempt to integrate the sociological with the psychoanalytic point of view, there is likelihood that the resulting classifications will combine the advantages of system analysis and depth psychology. Sociological concern with interaction patterns, small-group analysis, and role theory provides a safeguard against concentrating on a specific individual and thereby becoming involved in the intrapsychic conflicts of one individual only. In every human relationship, two psychological systems are engaged in long lasting transactions that can be understood only if both systems are considered as having equal claim to diagnostic attention. Concentration on one individual in diagnosis or therapy is based on the assumption that solution of the intrapsychic conflicts in one partner in a human relationship will have beneficial consequences for the solution of the intrapsychic conflicts of the other. Although such may be the fact in certain constellations, it cannot be taken for granted. Actually, it is interesting to note that practitioners in both psychiatry and social work have pointed out that the improvement of one family member sometimes results in the deterioration of another.[2] Although these clinical observations have never been contested, they have failed to receive the response they deserve. For a long time, they were disregarded in practice, and now, in a period of widespread experimentation with family therapy, conjoint therapy, and simultaneous therapies, they are not cited as reason or empirical basis for the desirability of these methods of treatment. It has long been the opinion of this writer that the refusal to heed the implications of these clinical observations and the later tendency to forget them are due to the inadequacy of the concepts used to safeguard the comprehensiveness of perception. Concepts of different degrees of abstraction have a tendency to force perception on the more concrete one. Dichotomies like those between the individual and his environment, the individual and his family, or a child and his parents operate under the perceptual principle of figure and ground. Of necessity, the phenomenon referred to in the singular becomes the "figure" and that representing a plurality the "background" of perception.[3] For this reason, concepts like interaction, social system, small groups, and life cycle of the family have a tendency to enforce consideration by the diagnostician and therapist of all human beings involved in these constellations. Sociologists work routinely with these concepts. They do so, however, without sufficient awareness of the influence of intrapsychic conflict, unconscious motivation, and ambivalence upon the nature of the interaction patterns they describe, the group processes they try to observe, and the performance of the social roles they try to classify and put into the perspective of social change.

Integrating these two points of view and the concepts to which they have led unfortunately produces a high degree of complexity. It vastly increases the number of phenomena to be considered and demands decisions about their differential impacts upon prognosis and therapeutic planning. This complexity presents anybody who demands such integration with the obligation of making it manageable for purposes of diagnosis and relevant for therapeutic planning.

In family diagnosis, it is convenient to classify the multiplicity of relationships into three subsystems: the marital system, the parents-and-children system, and the siblings system. Each of these three subsystems is composed of a plurality of interaction patterns: between husband and wife, between parents and children, and among siblings.[4]

Another and very important sociological point of view in diagnosing a family is based on the conception of the family as a small social organization that goes through various phases of development. Sociologists speak of the life cycle of the family,[5] and social workers frequently mention the differences in life tasks that confront families at different stages of their development. Again, it is convenient to distinguish a number of phases. First, there is that phase of the family life cycle reflecting the effort of husband and wife to form the basis of a new family system distinct from their background families. The next phase is usually that of child

Dimension of need complementarity	Function in marriage before arrival of children	Function in marriage and child rearing
Personal orientation	1. Providing a new and age-appropriate anchor of intimate association in place of parental anchor 2. Acceptance of nonpathological regression in partner 3. Security of receiving consideration and care 4. Security of sharing a spectrum of common interests	1. Permitting the other to fin additional anchors of intima association in children 2. Supporting each other in accep ing restriction of freedom to a cept nonpathological regressio because of presence of childre and protecting other again stimulation of regression throug interaction with children 3. Security of receiving consider tion and care 4. Security of sharing an increase spectrum of common interes through concern with childr« in daily living
Sexual sphere	1. Proceeding toward harmony in biological completion 2. Social permissibility of the experience 3. Coupling effect of 2. 4. Promise of realization of self through reproduction	1. Greater harmony in biologic completion 2. Social permissibility of the e perience 3. Coupling effect of 2. 4. Realization of self through r production
Economic sphere	1. Division of labor between earner and homemaker, with possible modification due to entrance of women in labor market 2. Provision of experience of tangible property through home 3. Promise of economic security through earning power of women	1. Division of labor more pr nounced due to demands of chi rearing 2. Provision of experience with ta gible property through home 3. Helping one another in copi with decreased economic securi resulting from expense of chi rearing
Ego strengthening	1. Help in learning spouse roles 2. According one another freedom to express individuality and help in maintenance of identity feelings 3. Support in maintenance of socially adaptive defenses	1. Help in learning parental rol and changed spouse roles 2. According one another freedo to express individuality and he in maintenance of identity fe ings plus protecting each oth against using children for wi fulfillment and identity 3. Continuation of support maintenance of socially adapti defenses

ASSISTANCE IN CRISIS OF TRANSITION

→

	Function in marriage and child leaving	Function in marriage after children have left
ASSISTANCE IN CRISIS OF TRANSITION	1. Permitting the other feelings of loss over departure of children and furnishing stimuli for re-orientation (redistribution of libido) 2. Renewed acceptance of non-pathological regression in partner and protecting one another against climacteric reactions to leaving of children 3. Security of receiving consideration and care 4. Security of sharing a spectrum of common interests through compensation for disappearance of children from contacts of daily living	1. Supporting other in continued search for new stimuli of re-orientation, including coping capacity with loss of spouse 2. Increased permissiveness with nonpathological regression 3. Changes in security of receiving consideration and care 4. Permitting one another a decrease in spectrum of common interests because preparation for loss of spouse requires divergent interests
	1. Support in the disturbance of oedipal repressions in the spouse due to sexual maturation of children of opposite sex 2. Social permissibility of the experience 3. Coupling effect of 2. 4. Promise of grandchildren	1. Support in decline because of psychological aging 2. Social permissibility of the experience 3. Coupling effect of 2. 4. Realization of reproduction beyond own children
ASSISTANCE IN CRISIS OF TRANSITION	1. Experimenting with modification in patterns of division of labor 2. Provision of experience with tangible property through home 3. Increase of economic security through wife's renewed availability for gainful employment because of freedom from demands of child care	1. Further experimentation in division of labor and employment in preparation for retirement 2. Acceptance of reduction of home scale 3. Helping one another to accept decrease of economic security because of difficulty in finding new employment or because of reaching retirement age
	1. Help in learning changed roles in both spheres 2. According one another freedom to express individuality and help in maintenance of feeling of identity 3. Support in maintenance of socially adaptive defenses plus tolerance for loss of socially adaptive defenses and guilt feeling over death wishes	1. Help in learning changed spouse roles and becoming ready for bereavement roles* 2. According one another freedom to express individuality and help in maintenance of identity 3. Increased support in maintenance of socially adaptive defenses plus tolerance for loss of socially adaptive defenses and guilt feeling over death wishes

* Usually not practical because of repression of death thoughts.

bearing and child rearing. The third is the one in which the children leave the home; it comes to an end when the last child has established himself independently. There follow a phase in which marriage partners again present a two-person family and ultimately one in which only the husband or the wife is the survivor.

Within every subsystem and at every stage of the life cycle, there exist various dimensions of complementary need that serve two purposes: satisfaction in the present and preparation for the future. As the purpose of this paper is to introduce a discussion of the psychotherapies of marital interaction, only the marital relationship will be discussed from these various points of view.

In all phases of the family's life cycle, the dimensions of need complementarity in the marital relationship can be classified as interpersonal reorientation, sexual and economic spheres, and ego strengthening,[6] although they may differ in weight and content as the family passes from one developmental phase to another. Chart 1 is an attempt to show interaction patterns in these various dimensions and their changes from stage to stage of the life cycle. It will be noted that every phase is separated from another by a crisis of transition, in which the function of the marriage partners is visualized as mutual assistance. This systematization follows Gerald Caplan's conception of the strategic meaning of crisis for development.[7]

The interaction patterns of healthy marital relationships in the various phases of family development are based on the assumption of satisfactory exchange of relationships,[8] in which marriage partners function at the same time as sources and recipients of marital need satisfaction.

The interaction patterns in marriage, as in other human relationships, can, however, be violated in various ways. The marriage partners may suffer a condition of mutual starvation. In any one dimension of need, complementarity, they may fail to give each other the satisfaction compatible with conditions of health. They may fail to provide each other with new anchors of intimate association and may thus fail to help each other in psychological separation from their respective parents. They may fail to give each other sexual gratification. They may fail each other in accepting the division of labor between earner and homemaker in family life. They may destroy each other's socially adaptive defenses. Such failures usually represent the contents of the presenting symptoms. In any one of the forms of therapy in which both marriage partners are being treated, there comes a point, however, at which an obstacle to improvement on a deeper level is encountered. This obstacle frequently reveals itself as an operation of the exchange principle on a more regressive or arrested level.

Failure to furnish each other with new and age-appropriate anchors of intimate association may permit maintenance of unresolved oedipal ties to the parents of the spouses. Failure in the sexual sphere may permit regressive gratification like masturbation or acting out, as in adultery. On the other end of the developmental spectrum, denial of permissiveness with nonpathological regression may permit the spouses to aid each other in refusal to acknowledge their physical and psychological aging and may thus aid them in an unrealistic attempt at permanence in interpersonal and intrapersonal maturity. This point suggests that an integrated approach to diagnosis of marital interaction patterns will have to cover overt dysfunction as well as covert function of the exchange principle. Such failures of the spouses to perform age appropriately and phase appropriately during the life cycle of the family furnish a measure of psychological justification for arrested or regressive interaction. They thus present a "double bind" situation not only in terms of communication as explored by the Don Jackson[9] group but also in terms of co-operation.

The obstacle to the improvement of marital interaction can also, however, lie in a disharmony between the ego ideals of the spouses and the social-role demands they are asked to meet due to cultural change. The marital dysfunction may not be compensated for by secondary gratification catering to the needs generated at early levels of develop-

ment. It is possible that the four basic forms of dysfunction
in interaction patterns are the result of failure in establishing harmony between residual self-demands to live up to
the requirements of obsolete self-images and new role
patterns.

Our times are characterized by a distinctive trend toward
exchangeability of men and women in the performance of
social roles formerly exclusively assigned to one or the
other sex. Fathers are taught to feed and bathe infants,
wives are taught to equal men as wage-earners in the same
lines of work, and both husband and wife are taught to
share the burden of social-role performance rather than to
divide it in terms of sex-specific role allocation. In consequence, sexual identification is reduced to the biological
sphere and to token behavior in the social sphere. Women
who are aware of their power to support the family and of
their enforced authority in the home due to the fathers'
absence often try to dress as if they were sex objects forced
to attract men by the symbols of their sexuality rather than
by the resource capacity in human relations that they represent. Men wash dishes but refuse to wear aprons. They can
accept the higher living standard and retirement security
provided by the earning power of their wives but find maintenance of their self-images in the fact that their take-home
pay is higher than that of their wives. They may be tempted
to try to prove their virility by acting out sexually rather
than by trying to elicit and stimulate sexual responses in
their wives. When faced with the problem of sharing home
maintenance, wives may be tempted to maintain their feminine self-images by combining the burdens of earning adequate incomes and keeping up adequate standards of home
care. Husbands try to keep up their self-images by refusing
to carry out tasks of home maintenance or child discipline
that their wives would like to see them perform. And basically there is interpersonal conflict because, when the principle of sharing role performances replaces the principle of
the division of labor, the attitudes of accounting and balance
are introduced into a social system. Again, covert and overt

need satisfaction and frustrations create "double bind" situations. A husband may refuse to let his wife share the economic burden of supporting the family and may thus introduce dysfunction into the economic dimension of the marital relationship on the manifest level. Covertly, he may fight for the maintenance of his masculine self-image. Offer-

Chart 2—"DOUBLE BIND" SCHEMA FOR DIAGNOSIS OF
INTERACTION PATTERNS

Presenting Symptom	*Nature of dysfunction*	*Obstacle to improvement of interaction (covert gratification of regressive or arrested needs)*
Violation of manifest exchange principle	1. Nongiving on both sides	I. 1. Mutual nongiving—legitimation of receiving from sources other than marriage partner, including the closing of the system
	2. Nongiving on one side	2. One-sided nongiving—maintenance of self-image through *gestalt* of unrewarded performance on the part of one and maintenance of self-image through successful exploitation on the part of the other
	3. Mutual infliction of damage	3. Mutual destruction—gratification of death wishes by both partners or gratification of desires for punishment by both partners
	4. One-sided damage	4. One-sided destruction—gratification of one partner's desire for punishment and gratification of the other's death wish
		II. Lack of model for ego ideal corresponding to social role demands resulting from cultural change—applicable to all types of dysfunction

ing him help in accepting the realities of the modern labor market may deprive him of the gratification of being an adequate male in his own eyes.

Limitations of space and reader tolerance for schematic presentations make it impossible to present a chart in which disturbances in all the functions represented in Chart 1 are shown as possible "double binds" with covert functions, or as conflicts between ego ideal and role demands, but a partial chart may stimulate further effort at systematization.

The possible illustrations to which this chart could be applied are practically unlimited, but one may be in order here. It could be assumed that a woman who does not want to have children and who refuses her husband intercourse without precautionary measures would exploit him in the area of promise of reproduction in the sexual dimension in either phase 1 or 2 of the marital relationship. The man may consciously complain of this treatment but may unconsciously enjoy the freedom from the responsibility of providing an adequate income for wife and children and of sharing his wife's attention with the children.

After the nature of the "double bind" is explored, the therapist's task is to offer himself as an ally to the age- and phase-appropriate side of the ambivalence of the marriage partners. He will be able to be effective in making such an offer only if he has himself overcome the pull of the arrested or regressive phases of need satisfaction presenting the content of the secondary gains that the marriage partners derive from their failure to function in age- and phase-appropriate manners.

In the area of conflict between ego ideal and role demand, identification with one's own sex and the nature of involvement in performance of life tasks are greatly handicapped by the failure of the helping professions to rethink the concepts of masculinity and femininity for themselves as well as for their patients. It has become a ritual to accuse wives of being dominant, aggressive, and frigid and husbands of being submissive, passive, and sexually either unresponsive or acting out. Therapeutic goal setting is also ritualized in the recommendation that the husband should be strengthened and that the wife should be helped to accept her own sex. These two rituals imply failure to provide the helper himself as well as the patients with socially feasible and morally acceptable goals. Here the task of the therapist will not be to present a model of age- and phase-appropriate conquest of ambivalence but to formulate new models of masculinity and femininity with which people can live in our time without being exposed to the "double bind" between modern ego demands and anti-quated ego ideals. This task, however, is one for which the helping professions are poorly prepared. It requires creativity instead of liberation, fashioning of civilization rather than helping people to cope with its discontents.

In summary, the task of the professional person called upon to help in cases of marital conflict seems to encompass the following steps:

1. identification of the dimension, content area, and phase aspect of dysfunction in the marital relationship;

2. identification of the obstacle to improvement in terms either of arrested or regressive secondary gains or, in the absence of agreement, between ego ideals and social-role demands of modern times.

3. offering himself as an ally to the age- and phase-appropriate side of the ambivalence in the marriage partners or as a representative or designer of a changing culture with new ego ideals.

The question for research or clinical demonstration will be the question of differential effectiveness among the approaches suggested by the concept of the "six Cs" in relation to specific obstacles to dysfunction in terms of secondary gains or obsolete ego ideals.

NOTES

1. Bernard L. Greene, Alfred P. Solomon, and Noel Lustig, "The Psychotherapies of Marital Disharmony," *Medical Times,* 91 (March, 1963), 243-56; Helen Harris Pearlman, "Family Diagnosis in Cases of

Illness and Disability," *Family Centered Social Work in Illness and Disability: A Preventive Approach* (New York: National Association of Social Workers, 1961), p. 8; Dorothy Aikin, "Family Diagnosis and Treatment: Some Implications for Casework Practice," paper presented at the National Conference on Social Welfare in Cleveland, May 22, 1963 (in process of publication).

2. Mildred Burgum, "The Father Gets Worse: A Child Guidance Problem," *American Journal of Orthopsychiatry*, 12 (July, 1942), 474; Gordon Hamilton, *Psychotherapy in Child Guidance* (New York: Columbia University Press, 1949), p. 282; Nathan W. Ackerman and Peter B. Neubauer, "Failures in the Psychotherapy of Children," Paul H. Hoch, ed., *Failures in Psychiatric Treatment* (New York: Grune & Stratton, Inc., 1948), pp. 86-8; John Bowlby, "The Study and Reduction of Group Tensions in the Family," *Human Relations*, 2 (1949), 124; and Ross Victor Speck, Clinical Director of the Eastern Psychiatric Hospital, Philadelphia, Pennsylvania, (verbal communication to author).

3. Otto Pollak, *Integrating Sociological and Psychoanalytic Concepts: An Exploration in Child Psychotherapy* (New York: Russell Sage Foundation, 1956), pp. 198-211.

4. Pollak, "Design of a Model of Healthy Family Relationships as a Basis for Evaluative Research," *Social Service Review*, 31 (December, 1957), 369-75; Henry Freeman, "The Parts that Make Up a Family," *Understanding Family Dynamics* (Pittsburgh: Family And Children's Service, June, 1960 [mimeographed], pp. 1-52.

5. Paul C. Glick, "The Life Cycle of the Family," *American Sociological Review*, 12 (April, 1947), 164-74.

6. Pollak, "A Family Diagnosis Model, Proceedings of the Conference on Family Diagnosis," *Social Service Review*, 34 (March, 1960), 19-31.

7. Gerald Caplan, *An Approach to Community Mental Health*, (New York: Grune & Stratton, Inc., 1961), pp. 18-20.

8. George Caspar Homans, *Social Behavior: Its Elementary Forms* (New York: Harcourt, Brace & World, Inc., 1961), pp. 30, 181ff.

9. Gregory Bateson, "Formal Research in Family Structure," Ackerman, Frances L. Beatman, and Sanford N. Sherman, eds., *Exploring the Base for Family Therapy* (New York: Family Service Association of America, 1961), pp. 136-40.

3

COUNSELING COUPLES IN CONFLICTED MARRIAGES

Emily H. Mudd and Hilda M. Goodwin

*Professors Mudd and Goodwin and their colleagues have written exten-
sively on marital counseling. The Marriage Council of Philadel-
phia* has become a model for the rest of the country. In counseling, the aim of therapy is to bring about an adequate adaptation
to external reality with its work and relationship demands. Counseling is primarily concerned with the ordering of the environment. Doctors Mudd and Goodwin again present their pragmatic
contributions to this operational approach.*

The methods and techniques of marriage counseling, along
with other preventive therapeutic efforts for the modification of human behavior, are being challenged by new
knowledge from the social sciences, from biology, and from
dynamic psychology. Static concepts are less popular, sound
and constructive experimentation more acceptable. We turn
to clinical experience to determine the extent to which
generalization can be substantiated and to explore one way
of working with conflicted marriages.

Through the years the word "counseling" has been used
to describe a wide variety of activities, and accordingly it
carries different connotations to persons of different backgrounds and experience. For our purposes, "professional
counseling" has certain definite attributes. It is a learned
art, in which a professionally trained person has acquired
basic knowledge, attitudes, and skills, which he has integrated in a disciplined capacity to apply himself therapeutically within the immediate experience of the interview.
Basic knowledge in marriage counseling, we believe, in-

---

*A nonprofit community organization affiliated with the University of
Pennsylvania, School of Medicine, Department of Psychiatry, Division
of Family Study.

cludes understanding of human growth and development, of the dynamics of personality, and of motivation; some understanding of social and cultural factors and their impacts on the individual; and an understanding of the reciprocal nature of interaction patterns in marriage. In addition, basic knowledge includes a disciplined awareness of one's own biases and attitudes as they may affect the counseling situation and an ability to use basic counseling skills. Arbuckle has pointed out that there is a fundamental relationship among the counselor's self-concept, his value systems, and what actually occurs within the counseling situation. He indicates that professional preparation can be effective only to a point unless the well worn phrase "Know thyself" becomes an intrinsic part of professional preparation. It is essential that the counselor be aware of his own attitudes, role expectations, and ethical or moral convictions concerning marriage. He should also have an adequate understanding of the biological and psychological attributes of sexuality, and he must be comfortable with his own sexuality.

The Marriage Council of Philadelphia and the Division of Family Study have had more than a quarter-century of experience in working with troubled marriages. From early days, it was part of the philosophy of the Council that marriage was composed of two people and that every effort should be made to involve both partners in counseling. This approach is implicit in the client's first contact with the agency and is reiterated and reinforced by the structures that have been evolved as framework for the counseling process. In more than 75% of all cases, both partners have been involved in the counseling. Although the legal and institutional aspects are recognized as part of the totality of marriage, our emphasis in counseling engaged or marital partners has been on marriage as a reciprocal human relationship between two people, each with a characteristic way of relating to other people in an effort to meet his or her own needs. The diversity and depth of need that any two individuals bring to marriage are complex and tend to change with greater maturity and with altering life situations. Satisfaction or dissatisfaction with the marriage thus depends upon the balance in the meeting of reciprocal needs and on whether or not the relationship is sufficiently flexible to change as the individuals and their environment change.

The goal of marriage counseling is to help each partner, through his relationship with the counselor, come to some awareness of the appropriateness or inappropriateness of his own feelings, attitudes, demands, expectations, and responses, as they are related to his marriage, and to help him resolve or handle more adequately those factors that are causing trouble within the marital interaction.

The focus in counseling is thus on learning to understand the reciprocal interaction between the two partners, rather than on each person's intrapsychic conflicts, as in individual therapy. By "interaction" we mean the unique day-to-day patterns of behavior, of response to stress and problems of verbal and nonverbal communication and interchange, of agreement or disagreement on roles, values, and goals. We have learned through our work that each partner brings to the marital relationship not only his usual pattern of attempting to satisfy his own needs but also his way of reacting to needs in the other person. We recognize that the choice of marital partner may represent the convergence of many different motivations, some conscious and some on a preconscious or unconscious level, and that each takes into marriage some unresolved conflicts and needs from childhood. When the marriage relationship fails to afford satisfaction of needs or fails to meet them in ways to which the individual has been accustomed, conflicts develop, and a destructive spiral may be set in motion. This spiral leads to frustration and resentment, with breakdown in meaningful communication. It enhances failure to support each partner's personal identity, and as a result it fails to alleviate anxiety about oneself and the threatened loss of the marriage.

It is apparent that this type of counseling rests heavily

on the findings and insights of dynamic psychiatry for its basic approach to and understanding of human motivations and conflicts and that it also uses significant concepts from the sociocultural fields.

Certain basic assumptions are implicit in our definition of the counselor's role and the goals of counseling: that each individual has within himself the capacity, perhaps latent, to experience, become aware of, and understand those aspects of himself and his behavior that create pain and difficulty for him in his human relationships; that each person has a motivating force toward growth; that these capacities can most readily be made available for the client's use in an anxiety-reducing, understanding, and reality-oriented relationship; and that the client has the right to make, within wide limits of possibility, the choice of what he desires and can live with.

There are a variety of ways in which marital counseling is offered at The Marriage Council of Philadelphia: Through experience with varying approaches, the staff has found it more helpful in the majority of cases to have the two marital partners work with one counselor, rather than having each work with a separate counselor. Each partner is seen separately in weekly interviews of approximately fifty minutes each, and joint interviews are held as part of the application process, at intervals jointly decided by clients and counselor, and at the end. More recently, in a very few cases, the agency has experimented with counseling the two partners jointly throughout the entire period. It is also possible, after an initial period, to offer the choice of group marriage counseling, in which husband and wife are members of the same group conducted by the joint leadership of a man and a woman counselor. It has been our experience that having one counselor work with the two partners offers distinct advantages to the counselor, who thus has an opportunity to experience in a more direct way the complementary nature of the marital partners' personality patterns and the destructive ways in which they may be reacting to each other. From the point of view of the partners, this coming together for help with their marriage may be the first occasion on which each is involved in an attempt to solve their problems in a co-operative way. When one partner applies for counseling without advising his partner of his intention or when he does not plan to involve the partner, this unreadiness to follow the plan the agency has found most helpful becomes part of the content and focus with which we may work in the early interviews.

A definition of the counselor's role, as we see it, includes the assumption that ability to help the client rests on the capacity of the counselor to establish and sustain an understanding and compassionate relationship; to see the client realistically without undue judgment or rejection; and to move with him as slowly as necessary in his struggles to solve his problems. In marriage counseling, we believe that the counselor's role involves the capacity to relate to the two marital partners in an impartial, unbiased, receptive, and responsive manner, utilizing the immediate "experiencing" of each partner as a resource for understanding more deeply the patterns of interaction within the marriage. We recognize the basic importance of the counselor-client relationship as the medium through which help to the client flows and the process of problem-solving takes place. We also recognize that in some situations change takes place through this relationship, even though there has been minimal use of clarification and insight.

In marriage counseling, it is especially necessary that the clients have trust in the confidential nature of the relationship with the counselor and the agency from the beginning. It is very important that each partner have confidence in the counselor's integrity and so be able to share and discuss feelings, attitudes, and behavior with candor and freedom, knowing that what he or she shares will not be passed on to the partner without specific permission.

It has been our experience that most couples come to the agency for help at a point of crisis or additional stress that cannot be handled by the resources previously utilized. Efforts are made to offer initial appointments within a short time, even if assignment for continuing counseling has to be delayed. We have found that motivation to seek help is higher at points of crisis or stress and that conflicts may be more easily dealt with before a destructive pattern for handling the difficulty has become established.

Each partner is asked to complete a "Background Schedule" and a "Marriage Adjustment Schedule" prior to his initial interview with the counselor. The Background Schedule covers biographical data but includes questions about the person's early relationships and experiences. It may awaken the client to the fact that his difficulties predated the marriage.

The marital partner seeking help is deeply involved with himself and is often caught in a mass of undifferentiated feeling toward the partner. Questions on the Marriage Adjustment Schedule are designed to reveal feelings of the client and his partner about the affectional aspects of marriage, the degree of companionship, major areas of disagreement, in-laws, and division of responsibility in the home, as well as what the client sees as the major difficulty and ways of resolving problems in the past. Emphasis is on mutuality in marriage, and, as the client struggles with his awareness or lack of awareness of his partner's similar or different feelings, he may begin to separate himself from this partner enough to begin to acquire a different perspective on the marriage.

During the interview, the counselor takes responsibility for focus and direction, in order to meet the clients' valid dependency needs, that is, to know what he needs to learn to help them. Efforts are made to elicit the clients' feelings about being in a counseling situation, to learn how each partner defines the problems, when they began, any new or precipitating circumstances, how each has tried to solve the difficulties, how each thinks the partner views the problems, and what each would like to do about them. As they are able to express what role they assign to the agency and as the way in which the agency offers help is made clear in the interviews, the clients are able to externalize doubts and reservations about involving themselves with concrete pieces of agency structure: individual interviews of fifty minutes on a weekly basis, occasional joint interviews, working with the same counselor, and so forth.

The Marriage Council has always been a nonprofit, fee-charging service. Fees formerly were set on a sliding scale according to income and number of dependents. On January 1, 1964, however, because of rising costs and the agency's unendowed status, flat fees per interview hour were adopted, with group counseling costing half the fee for individual counseling. We feel that, in today's cultural scene, it is therapeutically advantageous to meet the clients as adult persons who carry responsibility for service requested on a value-for-value basis.

There is little essential difference apparent at the time of application between clients who come for marriage counseling and those who seek outpatient psychiatric help—the differentiation comes when clients recognize their problems in living and those on which they are at that moment willing to work. If it is found that a person's intrapsychic difficulties are of major importance, the client may be referred by the marriage counselor for individual psychiatric treatment. On the other hand, one of the marital partners may be involved with individual psychotherapy while the other is counseled at The Marriage Council, or both partners, with the psychiatrist's approval, may become members of a marital counseling group.

After the initial interview, assignment is made to a continuing counselor, exploration and treatment continue hand in hand, and various processes may be utilized, depending upon the personality structures and needs of the clients and the marital situation. Marriage counseling deals essentially with present relationships and conscious material, rather than with preconscious or unconscious material. Because we feel that life is a continuum, we believe it is important to gain an understanding of the courtship and early days of marriage, as well as of the couple's goals and expectations for the future. Occasional excursions into early history may be indicated as it becomes apparent that a particular aspect of a client's current difficulty is related to unresolved early experiences or relationships. As the client is able to separate these early experiences from the present marital relationship, he or she may be able to respond to the immediate experience more realistically.

The use of an additional structured schedule, containing simply worded questions on sexual behavior with multiple-choice answers, may help the client to discuss his sexual behavior, as well as that of his partner, at an earlier period of counseling than would be possible otherwise. The schedules thus make it possible to explore each spouse's feelings toward this aspect of their relationship—and what each believes the other's attitude to be. Many clients lack a vocabulary with which to talk about their sexual behavior patterns, feelings, and attitudes. We have found, on the basis of ten years' experience, that the use of these schedules (which were initially developed under a research grant from the United States Public Health Service) helps to allay the clients' anxieties about sexual matters, places a vocabulary at their disposal, and enables them to realize that other men and women have had, with variations, similar experiences.[1]

Psychological support; clarification of feelings, attitudes, and roles; perspectives on the implications of the problem; assistance in developing methods of communication with the partner; important other information indicated by the client's need and capacities; and occasional direct suggestions may be utilized.

Joint interviewing may be arranged at various points throughout the process of counseling. It is our belief that joint interviewing can be most effective if both partners have formed relatively stable, trusting relationships with the counselor. The counselor must assume responsibility for the establishment of structure, balance, limits, and focus during the interviews. He must have some understanding of the dynamics of each partner and of the patterns of interaction between them. It is essential that each partner be willing to participate in a joint interview, have adequate anxiety tolerance, and be able to exert at least minimal control of his hostility toward the other. Both must realize that each partner, supported by his confidence in the counselor, dares to discuss matters that may never have been aired before the other. Joint interviewing, we feel, should not be utilized if one partner is actively psychotic, has an extremely frail self-concept, or is very anxious and fearful of revealing himself to the other. Uses of joint interviewing are to enhance communication; to help the partners experience and recognize parts of their interaction that are destructive to their relationship; to help the partners express both positives and negatives and to deal with them together; to do some reality testing; to help partners to accept each other's needs they have not been able to recognize before; and to highlight that the problem is shared by both partners, rather than belonging to one alone.

For the counselor working within the triangular structure of counseling—one counselor with the two partners in individual and joint interviews—there are certain distinct advantages. He has opportunities to experience directly the feelings, attitudes, behavior, expectations, and goals of the individual partners as they relate to the marriage. He can begin to perceive, more swiftly than is possible when partners are treated by separate counselors, each partner's habitual pattern for meeting life and how each projects his own needs and drives into the marital relationship in either complementary or disruptive fashion. As the counselor listens in the individual interviews to each partner's hurts, disappointments, and projections, he can, without betrayal of the confidence of either, raise pertinent questions and comments about the partner's interpretation of the spouse's feelings, attitudes, or behavior. The fact that the counselor is having interviews with the other partner can be dynamic, not only in bringing into the immediate counseling relationship the individual partner's problems with competition and distrust, but also in the necessity it may place on the individual partner to strive for greater honesty with himself because of his awareness that the counselor knows and hears the other partner's side. Finally, the inclusion of both partners in a counseling relationship with the same counselor and concomitant focus on the social reality of the marital interaction help to regulate, to some degree, the intensity of the counseling relationship with each, to militate against the counselor's overidentification with either, and to avoid arousing excessive anxiety in either partner. Problems of transference and countertransference are then held to a level suitable to a counseling rather than to a psychotherapeutic relationship.

A final joint interview, set up three or four weeks in advance, concludes the counseling process. Treating the ending as a planned part of the counseling process enables the counselor to help each client to handle conflicting feelings aroused as separation from a meaningful experience begins: feelings of loss, guilt at wanting to end, fear of not being able to cope alone, and desire to be free and to affirm newfound strength. As the partners are helped to deal with these ambivalent feelings, they can make the ending their own, and for each partner the greater unity and communication can be a sustaining force as they move through the final stages of counseling toward a new beginning.

We have attempted to define counseling for marital couples. We have presented in detail the philosophy, underlying assumptions, treatment structure and method, and goals of one type of marriage counseling as it has been developed over twenty-five years at The Marriage Council of Philadelphia and the Division of Family Study, University of Pennsylvania. Some of the similarities and differences between this approach to marital problems and others discussed in later chapters are obvious. The process we have elaborated has been tested experimentally, modified, and changed on the basis of clinical observation and analysis of results. A staff exposed to an atmosphere of self-questioning, of evaluation, and of experimentation, in spite of the natural complacency encouraged by custom and habit, hopefully should be able to incorporate into its work the challenges of new knowledge from relevant fields.

NOTES

1. This schedule is copyrighted and, by permission of the United States Public Health Service, under whose research grant it was developed, can be furnished at cost by The Marriage Council to professional persons for professional use.

BIBLIOGRAPHY

Ackerman, Nathan W. *The Psychodynamics of Family Life.* New York: Basic Books, Inc., 1958.

Erikson, Erik H. *Childhood and Society.* New York: W. W. Norton Company, Inc., 1950.

Goodwin, Hilda M. "The Nature and Use of the Tridimensional Relationship in the Process of Marriage Counseling." Unpublished Doctoral dissertation, University of Pennsylvania, 1957.

Laidlaw, Robert W. "Marriage Counseling," Samuel Liebman, ed., *Understanding Your Patient.* Philadelphia: J. B. Lippincott Co., 1957.

McGowan, John F., and Lyle D. Schmid. *Counseling: Readings in Theory and Practice.* New York: Holt, Rinehart & Winston, Inc., 1962.

Mudd, Emily H. *The Practice of Marriage Counseling.* New York: Association Press, 1951.

————. "Psychiatry and Marital Problems," *Eugenics Quarterly,* 2 (June, 1955), 110-7.

Mudd, Emily H., and Hilda M. Goodwin: "Marriage Counseling," J. L. Moreno, ed., *Psychotherapy,* Vol. 3. New York: Grune & Stratton, Inc., 1958, 171-5.

Perlman, Helen H. *Social Casework.* Chicago: University of Chicago Press, 1957.

Saul, Leon J. *The Hostile Mind.* New York: Random House, Inc., 1956.

Sullivan, Harry Stack. *Conceptions of Modern Psychiatry.* New York: W. W. Norton Company, Inc., 1953

4

TREATMENT OF
MARITAL DISHARMONIES:
THE CLASSICAL APPROACH

Peter L. Giovacchini

Doctor Giovacchini, in his studies on symbiosis and object relationships, has made a valuable contribution to the psychoanalytic literature. He has pointed out the mutual adaptive qualities of various types of object relationship, emphasizing how the neuroses of two individuals complement each other. He concludes that there are striking similarities in the characters of persons involved in long-established mutual object relationships. In this chapter, he presents a thought-provoking essay on the "complications" of multiple-oriented therapy vis-à-vis individual psychoanalysis.

This book illustrates the continued and intensified interest in understanding the therapeutic process and its many innovations and applications. Marital partners and the subtleties of the relationship between husband and wife have been intriguing subjects since the beginning of civilization. Little wonder then that the basic family unit, beginning with Adam and Eve, should now come under psychoanalytic scrutiny.

The therapeutic approach to any specific problem or situation, if it is to be founded on scientific tradition, must have a theoretical rationale. This statement is true of psychotherapy in general. If the treatment of marital partners warrants consideration as a separate topic, then there must be particular aspects of a more general theory to be focused upon, aspects that will serve to highlight certain areas of the therapeutic process. In looking at the treatment of married partners from a psychoanalytic point of view, we must define it in terms consistent with a theoretical superstructure. Consequently, there is a need to examine both our clinical approach and the concepts underlying it. In a clinical science, as in any other science, there is a need for examination and re-examination, continued evolution, expansion, shifts in point of view, and widening horizons. Therapeutic ambitions rise and fall; treatment goals are constantly re-evaluated. Today there has been a movement away from what is considered the traditional or classical psychoanalytic approach. This shift has been viewed as a modification of the orthodox position, one that is characterized by humanistic interest and the recognition of practical realities. Changes in science are often associated with progress, and the spirit of exploration that goes beyond classical psychoanalysis is considered by many investigators to be a sign of development. Furthermore, the kind and number of cases presenting themselves to the psychiatrist and psychoanalyst have forced them to deviate from the so-called "standard" techniques. These deviations, which Eissler[1] calls "parameters" (a term that has become almost a classic concept in itself), are widely discussed not only by psychiatrists but also by social workers, psychologists, and other professionals who deal with the study of man. Other professional workers naturally have their own techniques, but the formulation of the parameter concept by the psychiatrist makes possible a co-operative study of such techniques. Even though the various professions may start from different points, there has been an attempt to formulate concepts with similar superstructures.

Parameters have caught our professional fancy. Still, before we can speak of deviations, we must know from what we deviate. Orthodox classical analysis, although often discussed, has never been thoroughly described. We speak of the analyst's impassivity, his mirror-like qualities, his avoidance of any human expression toward a patient, and a variety of other factors that focus upon objectivity and distance. Distance, however, has been viewed by many as coldness, and because of the many emotionally needy persons seeking help, it is believed to be an inappropriate reaction. Nevertheless, these types of description are superficial. The best we can say about them is that they are phenomenological. But we cannot define anything as complicated as a therapeutic approach only in terms of its phenomenology. The "classical psychoanalytic" technique has not received the theoretical attention it deserves.

Freud[2] emphasized that the interpretation of the transference neurosis was the essence of his approach and that anything else might be detrimental to analysis. It is quite obvious from Freud's writings and those of his biographer Ernest Jones,[3] however, that Freud related to patients in many ways that transcended interpretation. This point does not militate against Freud's dictum, and some of his papers read like primers and directions for psychotherapists, even though he could not practice what he preached. One wonders, though, if the innovator of the psychoanalytic method could not abide by it himself, whether or not it might be even more difficult for his followers. Still, his ideas require scrutiny from a scientific point of view, regardless of their difficulty of application. What followed had many paradoxical features, for some analysts blindly and rigidly adhered to his dicta or thought they did, without particularly understanding the underlying processes, whereas others like Ferenczi and Rank[4] introduced extensions, or so they thought, that were so sweeping that their roots were no longer recognizable.

The treatment of married partners is especially interesting because, in considering how the classical approach can be utilized, we can at the same time learn more about the underlying ego processes associated with this approach. Any clinical study can be valuable in augmenting our understanding of dynamic interrelationships—in this case, those that occur between patient and therapist. The latter relationship can be pivotal for our theoretical understanding of the therapeutic process. As the other contributors to this volume stress their own particular therapeutic approaches, I wish to emphasize that not enough is really known about what has been called a "classical psychoanalytic approach." Here, instead of considering techniques in addition to or as extensions of those already included in analysis, I wish to focus upon a better understanding of these already existing techniques. I also emphasize that I am speaking of the *analysis* of married couples. Another investigator may feel that other approaches are better in particular instances, and it may well be that analysis is not applicable or practical in such instances.

The expense and time-consuming qualities of psychoanalysis are serious limitations. Consequently, anything that may ease the burden on both practitioner and patient is welcome. The characterological problems that are so frequently seen today, according to many psychiatrists, do not lend themselves to a therapy that lacks so-called "supportive" elements. If, however, the therapeutic process were better understood as a process, our conception of what the patient needs and responds to might be expanded. Sometimes it is not possible to substitute another form of therapy, even though the effective form has serious practical limitations. As an analogy, a ruptured appendix must be treated surgically—even if surgeons are scarce or unavailable. Another approach could be disastrous. What I am about to discuss, of course, does not have "life and death" implications in the physical sense, and we know that there are many ways of helping people. I shall address myself exclusively to those aspects that deal with character structure in both a clinical and theoretical framework.

As I have previously remarked, classical psychoanalytic treatment is imperfectly understood from a theoretical point of view. The theoretical understanding that we have has not kept pace with advances in other areas of theory. I shall consider the psychopathology of married partners and its treatment in terms that are consonant with the recent advances in ego psychology.

The insights gained from ego psychology can help us understand the psychic operations involved in the marital relationship. In turn, the deep and intimate ties between two people can contribute considerably to our knowledge about the operations of the ego in general. Marital disharmonies therefore represent a clinical area that can be fruitfully investigated and hopefully can contribute to both a theory of therapy and a theory of structure.

Any study of the ego eventually leads us into a study of object relationships. Object relations have been somehow involved in all areas of ego psychology, including development, learning, defenses, and adjustive techniques. Married partners are a particular example of an object relationship. From the point of view of the individual, object relations are of crucial interest in the therapeutic setting. One can easily understand then how significant the patient's relationship with the spouse can be as an indicator of his basic characterological structure and psychopathology.

Here, insofar as our interest is in the therapeutic process, ego developmental factors will be noted but not emphasized; instead, the marriage will be scrutinized in terms of its adaptive potential in the face of individual psychopathology. How each partner adapts to the other's personality and neurosis is in line with our clinical interest. That there is something different or special about the marital relationship, as distinguished from other object relationships, seems clear even at first glance. In a person's development, many objects become significant, each being needed or reacted to in a circumscribed fashion. Initially, the mother represents a global object, but, with development, other persons begin to fill distinctive roles and must have particular functional significance. The spouse, representing a heterosexual object choice, would ideally be associated with ego transactions at the most differentiated levels of psychosexual organization. We should anticipate that psychopathology would be reflected in a special way in such an object relationship.

There is an old adage that "marriages are made in heaven." Psychoanalysis, because of its strict adherence to psychic determinism, takes issue with this proverb, unless heaven is defined in terms of psychic processes. When a person has developed sufficiently to be able to exercise some autonomy in selecting an object, then there must be reasons, arising from past relationships, that cause him to select a particular person. If the relationship is characterized by strife, is one of disharmony, then the likelihood that he has stumbled upon it accidentally is minimal. It becomes even less likely when that relationship is a conflicted marriage, in spite of the fact that many patients protest that they were not really aware of their spouses' undesirable personality traits, that they had been misled, or that the courtships were too short for them to make accurate assessments. One sometimes senses immediately the need of one partner for the other, although the surface picture may be chaotic, turbulent, and painful to both husband and wife. When such patients are analyzed, certain characterological features become obvious and indicate that, even in situations in which the courtships were short, the patients either manipulated their spouses or themselves into marriage and that the relationships were extremely meaningful for the preservation of their psychic equilibriums.

Psychoanalysis is a therapeutic technique, as well as a conceptual system. The transference neurosis, an entity that Freud[5] mentions in one of his earliest publications, is the analyst's most important tool. Its unfolding enables us to scrutinize microscopically the patient's character structure, as well as to make formulations about psychodynamic conflicts. We learn about the patient's infantile past and his early object relationships as the transference neurosis develops. In psychoanalytic therapy, there is an ego regression that corresponds to, although it is not identical with, infantile ego states. The patient projects onto the analyst archaic imagos of significant past objects. From this vantage point, the analyst scrutinizes the patient's orientation toward objects in a contemporary setting as they represent reflections of attitudes from infantile relationships.

One soon learns that there are many variables that determine the choice of one's spouse. The psychoanalysis of a married person reveals that unconscious determinants are highly significant in determining such a choice. Data from the psychoanalytic frame of reference cause us to emphasize that there is much more than mere contemporary significance in the attraction between two persons and that marital interaction is founded largely on infantile attitudes. I do not intend that this conclusion become the basis of a generalization for all marriages. Obviously not all married persons seek psychotherapy, and those who are seen by psychiatrists have emotional problems that may distinguish their marital relationships from those of people who are not aware of any need for help. The inductive process has its limitations, and what pertains to cases of psychopathology is valuable only in the clinical setting.

Still, the distinction between persons who admit the existence of emotional problems and those who never come to a psychiatrist's attention may not be the same as the distinction between psychopathology and normality. Extra-therapeutic experiences have often led us to believe that some persons not in therapy have serious emotional problems, sometimes greater than many patients have. These problems are also apparent in the marital relationship. Although it does not follow logically, many would not disagree with a conjecture that there are elements of the infantile, relatively speaking, in every marriage. I do not necessarily mean that there are elements of the psychopathological in every marriage, nor do I wish to convey the impression that these elements must be considered in value terms, negative or positive. What is crucial here is their adaptive significance.

Many authors have made generalizations about the psychopathology of married partners. Both Oberndorf[6] and Mittlemann[7] have commented that the neuroses of husband and wife complement each other and indicate that there is a dovetailing of conflictual and defensive patterns. Oberndorf has described such complementing in terms of both pregenital and oedipal orientations. In a previous communication,[8] I have extended these conclusions and emphasized the mutually adaptive qualities of the marital relationship. I thought of these relationships as being symbiotic in nature, using the term "symbiosis," as DeBary[9] originally did, to signify mutual dependence. Benedek[10] and Mahler[11] have extended this concept to the biologically significant relationship of the mother-child unit. In this relationship, the child's survival and psychological development are at stake, as are important potentialities of the mother with respect to her motherliness. The concept of symbiosis, as it is used in biology, emphasizes that the need of each organism for the other is equally vital. Naturally such a concept becomes more complex when applied to humans. Symbiosis as it pertains to the mother-child relationship would not correspond exactly to the biological concept in which the child needs the mother for survival. Even though the mother's need for the child may be intense, she has at her disposal a variety of other techniques to maintain herself. One cannot therefore consider these needs as equal.

In the marital relationship, however, I concluded that the partners' needs for each other are equal. If this conclusion is correct, the pattern is symbiotic in the true sense and different and distinct from the symbiosis of the mother-child unit. But the label is not important. What is significant is the psychic process itself and not what one calls it.

The mutually adaptive qualities that are found in marriages are clinically impressive. I have come to the conclusion that the nature and depth of psychopathology are identical for the husband and wife in a long-established marriage. A long-established marriage does not necessarily mean a well established marriage. Indeed, a marriage may be characterized by strife and turmoil and appear to be on the brink of collapse. Yet in spite of continuing misery, one senses how necessary the marriage is for each partner's psychic survival. The superficial adjustment, in terms of behavior, defenses, and general adaptations, may appear markedly different in each partner for one may present a picture of relative calm and equanimity, while the other may seem markedly disturbed. The underlying personalities of the husband and wife are similar, however. We find that their basic conflicts, their points of fixation and regression, and their general ego integrations are the same. For example, if the wife presents an obvious picture of fragmented schizophrenia, we can feel relatively confident that the husband, although phenomenologically better defended, has similar underlying disorganization and will, under certain circumstances, become as fragmented as his wife. In fact, very often the wife establishes an equilibrium similar to the one that the husband initially had. He, in turn, may break down in a fashion similar to the wife's previous disorganization.

The data for such conclusions come from several frames of reference. First, we are most impressed by the reactions of one partner when a separation occurs. The importance of the object relationship to the maintenance of psychic equilibrium in both partners is then dramatically highlighted. For example, a man in his middle forties had been married for fifteen years to an utterly helpless, dependent woman. She found the pedestrian tasks of everyday living overwhelming and would frequently withdraw into catatonic-like states, in which she was completely detached from the world around her. She was frightened of everything and found every one and every situation dangerous. There was a paranoid flavor to her thinking, insofar as she believed that people were out to destroy her. She also saw herself as a venomous, destructive person who would be better off dead. In contrast, her husband presented the picture of a very forcible and highly adequate personality. He was successful in his business, very much an extrovert, and related easily and comfortably to people. He did not seem afraid of anything and went through life with a persuasive charm. He consulted a psychiatrist, not because he felt he had any personality problems, but merely to receive advice on how to help and handle his wife. The psychiatrist thought it odd that the husband had permitted such a situation to exist for so long a period of time, but the patient was able to produce a series of rationalizations, all of which made him appear favorably in the light of his forbearance. He wanted advice on how to help and handle his wife, but, when it was suggested that she receive therapy, he balked. Institutionalization was also out of the question, and he rationalized this attitude with moral arguments, insisting that it was his duty to look after her even though it was painful. He insisted that his only desire was to help her and even went so far as to deny all hostile feelings or even mild irritation at the trouble she caused him. In spite of his strict surveillance of all his wife's activities, she managed to run away to some relatives in another part of the country. With their help, she was able to resist both his threats and entreaties to return. She went into treatment in that faraway city. Because of the therapy and because she was away from her oppressive husband, she improved considerably. When the husband learned of this improvement and became convinced that, no matter what he did, she was not going to return, he became acutely disturbed. He presented a picture of total helplessness, had innumerable crying spells, and, like his wife, found every situation threatening and frightening. His air of self-confidence and bravado disappeared, and, in its place, appeared an infantile disorganization, which led eventually to hospitalization because he was unable to carry on routine activities. As in his wife's previous condition, there were also many paranoid elements.

This case shows that, at least phenomenologically, both partners reacted similarly. The marital equilibrium had a protective function for the husband. The later disruption of this equilibrium showed that he had always had the potential for the same kind of disorganization as that of his wife. This case does not prove that their character structures were identical, but, on the other hand, it suggests that they may have been.

We note similar reactions when one partner dies. The survivor frequently marries a person who seems identical with the first spouse. This pattern is particularly impressive in the wives of alcoholics, who, although they may complain about their sorry lots in life and how trapped they are by their irresponsible, acting-out husbands, often marry other alcoholics shortly after the deaths of their first husbands. It is not uncommon to find a woman who has been married to two or three alcoholics.

Another area that suggests a similarity of psychopathology in married partners is the therapeutic setting. The evidence that, when one partner improves in therapy, the other partner soon develops symptoms identical to those the patient initially presented is impressive. Often, the spouse who initially felt that he did not need help is forced to seek therapy for himself if the marriage is to be preserved. In some instances, the marriages were founded on such neurotic bases that, with therapeutic improvement, divorces were inevitable. Such divorces frequently resulted in regression in the untreated partners, which may have been similar to the patients' initial symptomatic pictures. Our earlier clinical vignette also illustrates this point, but there are many instances in which such regression takes place without actual separation. The improvement of one partner upsets the previously established equilibrium, and the defensive compensations that the marriage has held for the other partner are no longer operative.

A very striking example was that of the wife of one patient in analysis, who succeeded, in a relative sense, in overcoming some of her phobias. She was afraid of crowds and social gatherings. Consequently, she was unable to go to parties. She was also afraid of being away from her home, and, because of these symptoms, she was virtually a recluse. Her husband complained bitterly because his business demanded that he entertain and be entertained. He blamed her for his having missed many business opportunities because he was unable to attend various social functions alone. Because of her he felt chained to the house. After his wife had been in analysis for a short time, his wife's therapist suggested that he also receive analysis. The fact that he acquiesced was in itself interesting because he claimed that there was no such need. Still, he seemed glad that such a suggestion had been made. His analysis revealed that he had phobias almost identical with those of his wife, fear of crowds and parties, of being too far away from a toilet, and so forth. His wife's symptoms served to keep him away from anxiety-producing settings, so that he never had to experience the phobias or even to admit their existence. Her difficulties served to maintain his self-esteem and to protect him from the painful recognition of shame-provoking, passive needs. The wife's phobias became an excellent rationalization for staying at home and not being aggressive or manly, qualities that were frightening to him because of severe castration anxiety. This patient maintained psychic equilibrium by utilizing his wife's symptoms to mask his own. His wife's relative improvement accelerated the recognition of similar conflicts within himself, and for a long period of time during his treatment his phobias became full blown, showing striking similarity to his wife's previous symptomatic picture. In this case, because the husband was in analysis, it was possible to reconstruct his infantile conflicts and to compare his psychodynamic and characterological constellations with those that the wife's analyst had formulated about her. Both analysts were impressed by the similarities of their conclusions.

The analysis of the other partner provides valuable data to support the thesis that there is a homogeneity to each partner's psychopathology in a marriage. I have often been astonished by the reconstruction that a colleague has given of a husband or a wife of one of my patients, about whose psychopathology he knew nothing, or by the similarity between his conclusion about his patient and my conclusion about mine.

In psychoanalysis, the transference neurosis is the most important investigative tool. In making formulations about object relations, it becomes extremely valuable, for crucial object relationships are re-enacted with the analyst and can therefore be studied microscopically in a contemporary setting.

The infantile basis for the choice of a mate is especially highlighted in the transference setting. As inevitably occurs in any analysis, the patient will at some time or other relate to the analyst as if he were the spouse. The relation becomes apparent in dreams and associations, but what is projected on to the analyst also contains an archaic infantile object imago. The surface form of such an imago may be that of the spouse, but its constituents come from the infantile past. This transference manifestation demonstrates that the meaning of a husband or wife for an analytic patient is, in large measure, derived from past object relations, and the patient reacts to his spouse as if the spouse were a person that had been emotionally meaningful to him as well as conflictual during his childhood. Cases in which patients react to their wives as if to nurturing mothers are commonly encountered by psychiatrists. Or a wife may have for her husband feelings that she originally had for her father or, in some instances, a younger brother or a son.

Clinically I am impressed by the fact that the patient often complains or describes the spouse in terms similar to his own self-description. He is not aware of these similarities, and often a considerable period of time has elapsed between the two descriptions, but it is nevertheless striking how similar they can be. The transference neurosis again becomes indispensable if one is to evaluate such similarities, for one sees a projection of the self-representation onto the analyst.

The transference projections are projections of early introjects. Insofar as what is introjected is first perceived by the ego and then incorporated, the quality of the introject must also have some qualities of the introjecting ego, at least those of the perceptual system. Jacobson[12] has described in detail the various self- and object representations (acquired introjects) representing different developmental phases. Although all introjects possess some aspects of the self-representation, some do so more completely than others. What is striking in marital partners when they project elements of the spouse onto the analyst is the fact that what is projected is also a self-representation. One notes, often in dramatic fashion, that the patient's self-representation is the essence of the transference projection. Everything that the patient unconsciously feels about the spouse turns out to be true of himself as well. Consequently, the spouse is viewed as an extension or as a replica of the self. This view would not necessarily prove that the spouse is actually similar in personality to the patient; it merely indicates that the patient's unconscious attitudes toward the spouse are similar to his attitudes to himself, that he needs to perceive the spouse in this fashion. Without the study of the transference neurosis, we should find it difficult to reach such conclusions. I shall therefore present another clinical vignette in order to demonstrate how the transference neurosis reveals that the projection of the archaic imago representing the spouse also contains the self-representation.

The patient, a middle-aged professional man, constantly complained about his wife during his analytic sessions. He thought of her alternately as a weak, vulnerable woman who was unable to carry on the routine activities of homemaking and child-rearing. She drank much too much, and, even though he did not consider her quite an alcoholic, he felt that she was close to becoming one. At other times, he saw her as an explosive, unpredictably aggressive woman who nagged and descended upon him with a fury that made him fear for his life. He filled his analytic sessions with such material, practically to the exclusion of anything that referred directly to himself. He was able to acknowledge that he had some responsibility for this marital chaos and that, in his own passive manner, he contributed to it, but, in spite of this ability to look inward, he continued to complain vociferously. The analyst, however, constantly directed the patient's attention to the defensive meaning of his complaints about his wife and attempted to demonstrate how he had elaborated them into a complex analytic resistance. From time to time, the analyst became aware of subtle similarities between many of the things that he said about his wife and some of his descriptions of himself. As the analyst interpretively elaborated on the possibility that his preoccupation with his wife's inadequacy might be a method of protecting himself against low self-esteem and to cover up his own feelings of inadequacy, he gradually began to relate more directly to the analyst.

At this point, he began having dreams in which the analyst was attacking him or berating him ·in the same unpredictable fashion that he had ascribed to his wife. In one dream, he was trying to raise himself from the floor but found it difficult because two people were sitting on his back. His associations clearly brought out that these two people were his wife and the analyst. In contrast to his previously mild-mannered, docile attitude toward the analyst, he now became vociferous and argumentative. The contents of his productions were similar to those at the beginning of the analysis, except that now he had considerable affect with them, insofar as he was directing them toward the analyst. He was reliving in the transference neurosis the same defensive attitude that he held toward his spouse, and both the dreams and associations indicated that the wife and the analyst, from an unconscious point of view, were now one.

To view these developments simply as defenses against low self esteem and feelings of inadequacy would give us an incomplete picture. Obviously, his feelings represented, among other things, projections of infantile attitudes as they related to archaic objects. One can raise the interesting question as to whether or not such must be the case. Might it not be true that he gave a fairly accurate assessment of the wife's behavior and personality and that he was reacting in a realistic indignant fashion to the many burdens and pressures to which she subjected him? Undoubtedly there was considerable accuracy in his appraisal of his wife, and there was some evidence to support his allegations. Still, from the therapeutic point of view, whether or not he was describing reality was irrelevant. No matter what his wife was actually like, his attitude toward her still represented, to a large measure, the projection of infantile attitudes and imagos. This fact became evident as he re-enacted the whole drama in the transference neurosis. Certainly, the analyst could not and did not represent in reality the type of person he described, yet he reacted to him with precisely the same feelings that he had reported concerning his wife. In fact, there was considerably more affect toward the analyst although his previous complaints about his wife had been affectively mild and had seemed to have a slight intellectual quality about them. I wish to emphasize, therefore, that, in spite of the reality situation, it is important to note the patient's feelings in terms of his own internal psychic *milieu* and also to note that there must have been very significant meanings to his complaints other than realistic ones.

The patient also related to the analyst with the same ambivalence he showed toward his wife. In addition to his attacks, there were periods during which he saw the analyst as competent and strong. At times, he described his wife as a person with considerable charm, beauty, and poise, who could be masterful and adept in a variety of social situations. Nevertheless, the predominant emphasis was a negative one.

The transference neurosis revealed the following genetic antecedents: The patient was the younger of a pair of identical twins. His brother was looked upon as the successful one, whereas, for a variety of reasons, the patient was viewed and viewed himself as the "black sheep." What he said about his wife and later about the analyst in the transference neurosis was an almost exact replication of what he reported that others had felt about him during childhood in a role into which, because of guilt and masochistic defenses, he had manipulated himself.

The transference neurosis also revealed that he was projecting various aspects of this self-image onto the analyst. At times, he had to externalize a hated destructive part of the self and then attack it. This behavior had a defensive meaning in preserving his shaky self-esteem and in preventing his being overwhelmed by loss of control of disruptive feelings. On the other hand, he could attempt to repair his damaged self by a Pygmalion type of relationship with his wife. Rescuing her (there were many "rescue" dreams) would be tantamount to restructuring a defective part of the self. During the transference neurosis, when he felt positive, he attributed omnipotent healing qualities to the analyst.

As is common among identical twins, this patient had a serious identity problem. As the concept of identity is a very complex one and tangential to the topic of this chapter, I shall refer to it only in terms of its equivalence to some aspects of the self-image. This patient demonstrated that his wife represented to his unconscious a projection of a hated, destructively cathected self-image or its counterpart (the other side of the ambivalence), a powerful omnipotent self-image. He therefore saw her as similar to himself. She may not have been, psychically speaking, the "same" as the patient, but we are constantly impressed with how often, when the defense mechanism of projection is used, the object chosen is so appropriate.

This patient felt that, to achieve an identity separate from that of his brother, he must destroy him. This situation was one of extreme danger because killing his brother also represented killing himself, for psychically he could not differentiate himself from his brother. He was then able to gain a modicum of individuation by a split in his self-image, which reflected a split in the fusion of twinship. The separation, which was characterized by the ambivalence between the hated inadequate and the rescuing omnipotent, was then enacted in childhood and determined the core around which his marriage was founded.

Granted that this patient is unusual because of his identical twinship, patients with identity problems are by no means rare. Erikson[13] believes that this type of problem is practically universal among adolescents, and study of character disorders and borderline states emphasizing ego defects also reveals how deeply disturbed the identity sense can be.

In any case, the transference neurosis highlights the person's need to find himself in the object, although, in a clinical setting, infantile and destructive determinants are stressed.

The psychoanalytic study of married partners, therefore, leads us to several observations. First, we often find similar or complementary defenses, implying that there may be similar underlying conflicts but not necessarily proving their existence. Second, when it is possible to resolve or at least partially resolve these defenses, we are struck by the similarity of the underlying conflicts in the married pair. This similarity is most apparent in the frame of reference provided by the transference neurosis. Third, in some cases, relinquishing˙ defenses causes reversal of behavioral roles. When this reversal occurs in the analytic setting, we once again find identical underlying conflicts in married partners. Finally, the reaction to separation in some instances also results in reversal of behavioral roles, and again we are able to note similar underlying conflicts.

These marriages are characterized by intense involvements of one partner with the other. The marital partner requires the total personality, including the specific character defenses, of the other partner in order to maintain intrapsychic equilibrium. In spite of bitter strife and turmoil, the marriage lasts, and even though it may seem constantly on the brink of divorce, the observer recognizes that divorce is unlikely. To distinguish such a total characterological involvement between the husband and wife, I shall refer to this type of object relationship as a *character object relationship*.

Not all marriages, however, fall into this category of object relationships. There is another group that I shall designate as *symptom object relationships,* which differs from the first group in that the marriage is transitory in nature and does not have the same depth of involvement characteristic of a character object relationship. Frequently such marriages result in divorce, and equilibrium, pathological or otherwise,,has never been firmly established. Once again we sense mutual need in such marriages, but it seems less intense than in marriages of the first type. We have the impression that the patient's spouse does not have a specific meaningfulness to him. Analysis reveals that the patient does not require the total personality of the other; he needs only a particular trait or symptom, and the marital involvement seems only a partial one. Other objects with similar traits or symptoms, although differing in many respects, could serve his defensive needs as well, and frequently such a patient has had several marriages in which the spouse had a common denominator, so to speak, and also great differences.

For example, a wife in her late twenties revealed that her husband was a weak, inadequate person. She brought this point up as an incidental finding and was not particularly concerned about him. Nevertheless, she gave an extensive description of his personality and painted a picture of a detached, withdrawn person using schizoid mechanisms and perhaps bordering of schizophrenia. This woman, on the other hand, did not seem so seriously disturbed. She had sought therapy because of a variety of hysterical symptoms, and the analysis finally reached the core of her conflicts, which were basically oedipal. At this stage of analysis, it was learned that she was in intense competition with her mother, who was said to be more beautiful than the patient and covetous of her heterosexual successes. The mother both intimidated the patient and made her feel guilty (at least such was the patient's perception). Consequently, her romances never worked out well; she was defeating herself in order to placate a disapproving maternal superego. She felt unconsciously that, in order to appease her mother, she must have a husband who was passive and inadequate, but the nature of his basic psychopathology was not important. As long as the man she married was not desirable, her mother would not want to destroy her and take him for herself. She managed to find a man who did not rate high on the marital market. At the time of treatment, she was in her fourth marriage, her three previous ones having lasted a year or less each. All her husbands were described as "weak characters" who were unattractive physically, lacked charm, and were shallow and intellectually constricted.

Still, there were significant differences among these men. Her first husband had been a gregarious, back-slapping salesman who bluffed and boasted in so obvious and gross a manner that no one failed to recognize his ineptitude. He never achieved status, and his performance was mediocre.

The patient considered him crass, dull, and materialistic, lacking in sensitivity, and a bore. In contrast, her second husband had been a high-strung, overly sensitive artist who reacted or overreacted to even the most trivial stimuli. His demeanor was usually depressed or angrily rebellious, and he valued aesthetic and intellectual pursuits. He was also a failure, however, lacked talent, and talked more about working than he actually worked. His colleagues thought him a "jerk," and the patient stated that he was physically repugnant, unkempt, and unwashed. The other two husbands also differed from the first two and from each other, but each was inadequate in his own way.

This patient emphasized the circumscribed defensive meaning of the marital relationship. The spouse was not considered as a whole object. She related to only one particular characteristic of the husband, one that she used to defend herself from destructive and self-destructive competitive feelings toward her mother. The need for such relationships was vital, but, unlike patients involved in character object relations, she had greater flexibility and could shift from one object to another. A relationship founded on such a symptomatic basis would be unstable; other attributes of the spouse's personality extraneous to the patient's needs would eventually make the relationship untenable. This patient could not relate to either hypomanic, depressive, or schizoid qualities. These types of personality orientation were modes of operation foreign to her, were ego dystonic, and therefore interfered with the establishment of a marital equilibrium.

Symptom object relations are also found in persons who are not predominantly oedipal in their psychosexual development. For example, a young and brilliant scientist was unable to explain his failure to achieve a satisfying marriage. He had been married twice before, and in his third marriage he found himself distressed because he was going to leave his wife. He vacillated in his feelings toward her, but even when very angry he was reluctant to separate himself from her. Although he wanted a divorce, he did not want to admit defeat again. Nevertheless, he found her behavior intolerable because of her unpredictable and sometimes violently explosive moods. She would, at times, reject him completely and react with great disdain to any affectionate gesture he might make, just as, at other times, inexplicably, she might behave in a seductive, warm fashion. She had had difficulties in other areas too—vocational, academic, and social—and had been in therapy for several years. Her therapist diagnosed her as suffering from a schizophrenic psychosis, one that could not permit her any involvement in an object relationship. On the other hand, her husband was an affable, outgoing person with many warm friendships and social contacts. The impression gained from his analysis was that of a moderately severe character neurosis with obsessive features but nothing so severe as to suggest psychotic elements. Nevertheless, his need for his wife seemed very strong, as had been his pursuit of her during courtship and his tenacity in the marriage, although it was obviously an impossible one.

His motivations became clearer, however, when his relationship with his mother was better understood. Her main characteristic was also unpredictability. She, too, was openly seductive toward the patient and on several occasions made overt sexual advances. At other times, she would be violently antisexual and would adopt the manner of an incensed Victorian. The patient was dismayed and confused and found himself in a position of helpless vulnerability. He felt that his very existence was at stake. In order to overcome his anxiety, he had to solve the riddle of the mysterious, unpredictable woman. He deliberately associated himself with disturbed women in order to repeat the traumatic experiences with his mother and master the danger. The mother later became overly psychotic and died in a state hospital.

The patient was preoccupied with problem-solving, a motif that had played a large share in determining his choice of profession. His need for his wife was not based on characterological similarity; rather she represented a challenge and a problem to him. Such a challenge, by its very nature, could be found only in a seriously disturbed personality. The descriptions he gave of his first two wives, however, indicated that they were quite different from his third wife. One sounded like a fairly typical hysterical personality with a good deal of acting out, and the other one seemed moderately depressed with self-defeating qualities. Still, when he finally left his third wife, she had very little reaction, and her usual equilibrium did not seem disturbed. What he sought was this one trait of unpredictability, which he found in this woman and in other women of diverse character structures.

This case and others like it indicate that the object relationship is determined chiefly by the patients' conflicts, which are different from those of the partners, as could be seen in this partner's relatively mild reaction when separation eventually occurred. Undoubtedly, the partners had their reasons for marrying the patients, reasons that we cannot ascertain because they have not been studied. Nevertheless, we can conjecture that the particular conflicts that motivated the partners to enter into the relationships were of different orders from those of the patients. In the second case, in which the wife was in therapy, it was learned that she had attached herself to the patient because of a helpless, clinging, dependent need, almost anaclitic in nature, and she, too, would choose any man that seemed to offer these nurturing qualities.

Even as far as the patient was concerned, the involvement did not seem to be one of the total personality. A specific area of conflict seemed to be the chief determinant of the object relationship, but this area did not include the main characterological features of his psychic structure. This distinction is analogous to that between a character neurosis and a symptom neurosis. Anna Freud[14] and her coworkers suggested that there is a marked difference between an object relationship that is needsatisfying and one that includes object constancy. The former will exist only as long as the particular need is satisfied, whereas the latter has positive integrative aspects in terms of ego development. Anna Freud, Hartmann,[15] and Kris[16] have recognized the role of intrapsychic conflicts in the formation of object relationships. If the patient's characterological features in their more total and diffuse aspects are the sources of interactions between the marital partners, then a total, deep, and constant involvement seems to result. If, on the other hand, an isolated area of the ego—a specific defense or symptom, for example—becomes the pole around which the relationship revolves, then the relationship is less vital for the partner's intrapsychic stability and turns out to be transient, as in our two examples. This type of object relationship is typified by a symptom or rather the manifestation of a symptom. It represents one manifestation among many, however, whereas character object relationships become axes around which transactions with reality are achieved and internal equilibrium maintained, indicating characterological rather than merely symptomatic involvement.

Insofar as married persons relate to each other either in terms of a symptom object relationship or a character object relationship, we can expect complications in their analyses, and because many analytic patients are married we may consider such complications as characteristic of the analytic relationship. In the therapeutic process, these complications manifest themselves as resistances. In a previous communication,[17] I described these resistances as unusual, in that they seem to be initiated by external objects.

Resistances stimulated by external objects occur in the analyses of unmarried patients too. Those occurring in the marital relationship have special characteristics because of the equivalent psychopathologies of the partners. We often note that, although the patient's spouse frequently has encouraged analysis and sometimes even insisted upon it, once the patient begins making progress, his spouse's attitude changes. The analysis brings about the disturbance of a previous marital equilibrium. Then the spouse reacts, at first subtly and later more openly, in a fashion designed to sabotage the analytic relationship.

An especially striking example of a therapeutic impasse brought on by a sabotaging spouse was the case of a recently married young woman who had sought treatment because of a variety of somatic complaints. Her symptoms centered around the respiratory system and consisted in difficulty in taking full breaths, feelings of suffocation, and hyperpnea, all present from childhood but increasingly severe since her marriage. There were also many characterological features indicating a basically infantile personality with a strong oral component. Her appearance was that of a naive and sexually unsophisticated person, one who was described by others and, especially by her husband as a "wide-eyed, cute little girl." Nevertheless, she could be disdainful and haughty, and underneath what seemed a dependent helplessness, she had the attitude of a tyrannical aristocrat. She felt superior to her friends, and, although her husband was a successful professional man, she believed that he was of inferior breeding and did not know how to treat her with the respect, delicacy, and consideration that she deserved.

The defensive nature of this narcissistic orientation became apparent during her treatment, which revealed an ego beset with feelings of inadequacy and dominated by insatiable oral, dependent demands. Her feelings of inadequacy were determined by sexual conflicts that threatened her feminine self-esteem. She was basically hysterical, and the physical symptoms represented conversion processes, but the hysterical aspect of her personality became apparent only after a long period of treatment that was mainly involved with pregenital, oral dependent strivings.

In spite of her narcissistic orientation, this patient's analysis progressed favorably, and she seemed to be sincerely trying to work through her infantile dependent demands. This effort was reflected in marked improvement in her behavior. She seemed able to integrate analytic interpretations and then to utilize insights to effect new adjustments in her daily life. She seemed headed in the direction of self-sufficiency and basic resolution of her Oedipal problems.

After about eighteen months of what had seemed to be a well progressing analysis, the patient reverted to her old dependent status. All her initial physical symptoms returned along with her haughty, whining behavior. She now showed a stubborn naïveté and refractoriness to all interpretations. Granted that this type of regression and resistance is not unusual in an analysis when deep layers of conflict are broached, this patient showed a tenacity that seemed peculiar, especially in the light of her previous receptiveness. If it had not been for unmistakable evidence of previous working through of conflicts, I should have believed her completely untouched by the psychoanalytic process.

Still she was able to bring up new material, which shed light upon the nature of this intense resistance. She began talking in more detail about her husband, whom she described as a successful, secure person. She was aware of her critical attitudes toward him, but, nevertheless, she saw him as a mature man with great strength and concern for her welfare. He was enthusiastic about her treatment and had in many ways helped her get started. He handled himself discreetly and never raised any questions about what was going on in her analysis, although he was extremely inquisitive and protective about all other aspects of her life. It seemed that he was studiously avoiding any discussion of her treatment, and, in general, he seemed to encourage her to grow up. In spite of her regression, which was manifested in her general behavior as well as within the analytic framework, he did not show the least sign of impatience or discouragement. This attitude was especially odd because the cost of his wife's treatment represented a sizable financial sacrifice, and he was not a particularly patient man. He could be cruelly critical, but toward the analysis he had never evinced any disapproval.

The patient, however, began to suspect ulterior motives in her husband's attitude and behavior. She discovered that he wanted to keep her infantile. For example, he enjoyed having her use baby talk, something that she had done frequently in the past. Since starting her analysis, she found it odious, but she continued because she was afraid of displeasing him. She was aware of his resentment when she stopped. He also encouraged her sexual naïveté. He liked to tell her obscene jokes, but he wanted her not to understand so that he could shock and tease her with the explanations. Although she understood the meanings of these jokes as well as he did, she assumed an attitude of naïve bewilderment. When she actually behaved incompetently, his attitude seemed benign, but she was able to discern that he was patronizing her.

Consequently, she made special efforts to appear incompetent, sensing his need to have her remain childish. He encouraged her initially to seek analysis because there were various aspects of her symptoms that were annoying to both of them. Nevertheless, he really did not want any basic changes, and his need to consider his wife as helpless and immature represented an overcompensatory defense against his own low self-esteem. This defense became apparent later when he himself sought analysis; his wife's improvement forced him to seek help.

As the patient began to understand her husband's needs, she found it difficult to adjust to such an infantilizing atmosphere. The analytic impasse gradually gave way, and she was once again able to continue with the analysis. This resumption necessitated some changes in her external adjustment, which forced her husband to decide between divorce or analytic assistance for himself. He chose the latter, and a new marital equilibrium was eventually established.

In such cases, the therapist may be led to believe that he is dealing with a difficult and sometimes intractable reality situation. This case involved a resistance for the patient, which was at times sufficiently subtle so that its intrapsychic implications could easily be overlooked.

Although there are, indeed, difficulties in external adjustments, they still offer reflections of each partner's personal neurosis. On the surface, the spouse seems to be responsible for the disruption of the treatment, but he can be effective only if the patient allows him to be. These patients utilize external objects to defend themselves against awareness of their inner problems. True, the other partners attempt to sabotage the treatment, especially if there has been any significant progress, for they feel threatened by any changes in marital equilibrium. Regardless of the many uncomfortable aspects of a marriage, aspects responsible for initiating treatment, any shift in the equilibrium seems threatening to the other person. Nevertheless, the patient also responds to the threatened equilibrium and may in turn become frightened of further progress because it means going on alone without the usual defensive props. Consequently, the patient may encourage the sabotaging aspects of the spouse and may then use this attitude as an analytic resistance.

One cannot therefore focus upon the external situation. This problem is still an intrapsychic one, to which, in many cases, the patient has contributed. On the surface, it seems as if the patient is trying hard to work through inner conflicts and is being attacked by an undermining, sadistic spouse. Such seems to have been the situation in the case of the young woman. Still, as we scrutinize the subtleties of the marital relationship, it also becomes apparent that she had manipulated her husband to react as he did. He felt threatened by her progress and the upset in the marital equilibrium, but so did she. She unconsciously recognized the vulnerability of some of his defenses and attacked him particularly in those areas. She contributed to his feelings of insecurity and stimulated him to intensify his defensive behavior. They were both serving their own needs, but she was able to use his reactions as a protective screen against deeper transference involvements.

Object relations are a facet of ego functions. One has to include them in any study of the therapeutic process. In a marriage, any changes in the marital equilibrium constitute changes in an important object relationship for both husband and wife. These changes affect each partner's psychodynamic balance. Conversely, any shifts in psychic structure are reflected in all object relations, especially the marital one.

Clearly, the development of the transference neurosis gives us an excellent vantage point from which to observe various shifts in object relations. From such observations, we can better evaluate the effects of deviations from the one-to-one aspects of the psychoanalytic relationship. In view of our interest in the therapeutic process, I am raising the question of the significance for the patient of conjoint therapy or collaboration with the spouse. From an analytic point of view, it is important to see how such a parameter either helps or hinders the usual unfolding of the transference neurosis. From a longer-range perspective, we must formulate some hypotheses about whether or not the analytic goal, that is, the resolution of conflict and ego structuralization, can be better achieved if the spouse is somehow brought into the treatment—or whether or not the situation is inordinately complicated by a collaboration that might be reacted to as an interference.

These questions cannot be answered simply by observing symptomatic improvement or remission. Phenomenological criteria are inconclusive and do not add to our knowledge. What may at one time appear to be improvement, behaviorally speaking, may represent an intractable resistance and may really indicate therapeutic failure. Similarly, what may seem a worsening of the patient's condition may actually be a reaction to the relinquishing of a defense and a step toward ultimate resolution. Although we are all interested in the welfare of the patient, there are many ways of helping people that are not part of our professional orientation. To study questions concerning the therapeutic process, we must stay within a consistent conceptual framework, and the phenomena observed, at least in the psychoanalytic setting, must be understood in terms of their transference implications.

To return to the transference neurosis, then, we note

that it highlights the significance of contemporary objects in terms of their relevance to infantile objects. A serial hierarchy of object imagos extending from contemporary objects to archaic forerunners is found in any object representation. If this point is kept in mind, we can see that it is meaningless to think in terms of one element's belonging to transference and another's belonging to nontransference. Every object relationship must have some transference element, just as any thought, wish, or impulse has its unconscious determinants. True, the relationship may be founded mainly on conscious contemporary elements, and the unconscious infantile contribution to the relationship may be minimal. In any psychoanalytical study, however, it is the latter factor on which we must concentrate.

The question can now be rephrased. In what ways will a transference neurosis be affected if the analyst has any contact with the marital partner? Although a relationship with the spouse may not seem to have any particular effect on the patient, a microscopic scrutiny of the transference neurosis indicates that something has happened to some aspect of the transference relationship. This point is obvious because the analyst's contact with the spouse is an event, a stimulus, and every stimulus must have some reaction. Of course, the quality of the reaction determines whether such contact is helpful or deleterious.

The clinical example given at the beginning of this chapter suggests that there comes a point in the analysis of a married person when he projects onto the analyst an imago of the spouse. It also suggests that the imago of the spouse is similar to an archaic self-representation. This projection therefore highlights the infantile determinants of the choice of mate, as well as the narcissistic factors involved in such a choice. During this phase of the transference neurosis, the analyst represents the spouse, and the spouse in turn represents an archaic infantile self-image. Insofar as there is a lack of distinction between the patient and the spouse from the point of view of intrapsychic structuralization, there is a fusion between the patient and the spouse. This fusion is reenacted in the analytic setting, and we note during this stage of treatment a similar fusion between the patient and the analyst.

We might justifiably raise the objection here that these conditions are artifacts caused by analysis itself and not necessarily indicators of a basic orientation or even a modality that might exist between husband and wife. What appears in analysis must, however, be present in the patient to begin with. One cannot introduce a mode of reaction into a person for which he did not have the potential in the first place. What we uncover in the analytic relationship are mechanisms that, although not obvious, contribute to the patient's pedestrian adjustments and determine the character of his object relations. The transference regression highlights archaic qualities that are nevertheless operative even when the patient is not in a regressed state. This point is similar to that about every impulse and acting having its unconscious determinants. The regressed transference neurosis reveals reactions that are the prototypes for later adjustments.

An object relationship that has such primitive elements as fusion embodied within it causes special problems for the resolution of the transference neurosis. We always find elements of fusion during initial stages of development, especially in the neonatal period. As we are dealing here with marital partners specifically, I wish to bring into focus the difficulties that are created when the patient-analyst fusion reflects the patient-spouse fusion. This topic would not in itself deserve special consideration. We are considering, however, the effect a relationship between the therapist and someone known to the patient might have on the therapeutic process. Consequently, the mechanism of fusion becomes important.

Let us consider the triangle of patient, therapist, and spouse from a conceptual point of view and relate it to various transference elements. To repeat, the patient projects an infantile self-image in the form of the spouse on to the analyst. This projection results in the patient's confusion of the spouse and the therapist. His reality-testing is impaired. If the therapist is having an actual relationship with the spouse, the patient's confusion of the two becomes intensified. He receives support for his distortions by the existence of such a relationship. The extra-analytic relationship with the spouse reinforces the transference projection. The specific nature of the patient's reactions to such a projection would depend upon the content of the inner conflicts. Our task is to determine whether or not such a reinforcement creates obstacles for therapy.

To clarify the nature of the transference, as reinforcement sometimes does, can be helpful. But the main question is whether or not the transference can be resolved. The existence of a transference neurosis is not necessarily helpful to analytic resolution. Transference does and must occur, but it must be an operable transference, one that can be eventually recognized by the patient for what it is. In a large measure, the capacity to distinguish between transference feelings and reality depends upon the patient's integrative abilities and his capacities for reality-testing. The analyst's role, however, is paramount because the patient's reality-testing can be obscured if the analyst has behaved in a fashion that reinforces the transference projection. It is beyond the scope of this discussion to consider the optimal conditions that the analyst might create for transference resolution. Still, if the analyst behaves in a fashion congruent with the patient's fantasies and goes along with the qualities that the patient has projected onto him, then it becomes obvious that the patient will find it difficult to make distinctions between what he has projected and the reality of the analytic situation. It will be more difficult for him to introject an objective, observing, benign, and interested analyst whose chief function is to understand what is going on within him. Such an introject augments self-observing tendencies and, through introspection, leads to the formations of insights that emphasize intrapsychic phenomena. If the analyst, on the other hand, behaves in a fashion that is similar to the role that the patient has ascribed to him in the transference projection, then the formation of an observing introject does not occur. Instead, the patient will react toward the analyst as if he really were an archaic object imago.

If the analyst behaves in a fashion that corresponds to the patient's fantasies, then both the patient's and the analyst's abilities to view the object relationship of the transference neurosis as an intrapsychic phenomena are impaired. They both respond to what they consider to be reality elements. If the predominant transference results in fusion of the patient, analyst, and spouse and if the analyst has an actual relationship with the spouse, then the boundaries among these three persons become indistinct. The analyst's function is to help the patient be objective about his inner feelings. He attempts to show him that these feelings represent archaic reactions and fantasies. This task becomes increasingly difficult if he behaves in a fashion that reinforces the fantasies.

Ego boundaries become blurred, and the patient no longer feels himself a separate and distinct entity. To be fused with the spouse-therapist may give him unconditional security or cause him to feel helpless and vulnerable. The patient's reactions depend upon whether he is projecting an omnipotent wish fulfillment or a destructive rage onto the analyst, these two reactions not being mutually exclusive and usually alternating.

One might object at this point that this type of patient is an example of exceptionally severe psychopathology and that generalizations about therapeutic approaches cannot be made from a particular clinical group. I agree with this position, but many have emphasized the need for more varied approaches because the patients they have encountered have not responded well to traditional techniques. The reason offered for such a lack of response is that these patients are too sick to be treated in terms only of their intrapsychic conflicts and that some degree of environmental manipulation and support is required. It is precisely the type of patient who shows such primitive mechanisms who has been considered from the point of view of "marital therapy," and it is this type of patient who is most likely to develop difficulties in transference resolution if the analyst steps outside the analytic situation.

Furthermore, regressed ego states characterized by fusion occur in cases that do not show serious characterological defects. Such states occur as results of the regression set in motion by the analytic procedure and become manifest in the transference neurosis. Returning to a hierarchical concept of object relations we should expect to find a pre-object fusion state at the primitive end of the spectrum. Insofar as every relationship contains all elements of its development, even the most mature object relations contain some degree of earlier adaptive techniques. The latter may come to the fore in deep transference states and may lead to coɪ iplications if the analyst has reinforced the fusion with extra-analytic relationships.

The main element of transference resolution consists of the patient's recognition of the archaic nature of his transference feelings. He learns not only of the infantile qualities of his feelings but also that he has projected them on the therapist, thus coming to separate the therapist as therapist from a significantly emotional figure from his own childhood. The resolution of this specific transference state would result in recognition of the projection of an infantile self-representation embodied in the spouse on to the analyst— and the fact that this view of the analyst is a projection.

Boyer[18] made a point of not communicating with the relatives of thirteen severe adult schizophrenics, and Weiss[19] and Anthony[20] similarly refrained from consulting the relatives of their child patients.

What are the implications, then, of an extra-analytic relationship with or simultaneous treatment of the spouse in terms of the transference neurosis and the regressed ego state of fusion among patient, analyst, and spouse? What are some of the factors that enable the patient to discriminate between what is occurring intrapsychically and what emanates from the external world? In any analytic relationship, the patient, because of regression, reverts to infantile methods of relating to the therapist. Among the techniques utilized is introjection, and the patient introjects the analyst during many phases of the transference neurosis. The nature of the introject is multiply determined and has many facets essential for distinguishing between what is transferred and the object of transferences. The natural tendency of a patient who has fused the self-representation with the spouse-analyst is to confuse internal (introjects) and external reality. Ego boundaries are relatively nonexistent, and there is difficulty in maintaining a separation between self and objects.

Nevertheless, if the analyst has maintained his individuality, so to speak, an individuality that is determined by his adherence to the analytic role, the patient will introject some elements of it. By "analytic role," I do not mean distance or impassivity. Rather, I am describing the analyst's willingness to understand what is going on within the patient, instead of taking sides in his intrapsychic conflicts, and to feel that there is something within the patient worth understanding. This attitude provides a structuring experience for the analysand, one that strengthens his self-esteem. Inherent in the desire to understand is a respect for the patient's autonomy and his developmental potential. The analyst also conveys a nonanxious orientation in his response to the patient's infantile needs and conflicts. All these elements compose the analytic attitude, and to some extent they are introjected.

If the analyst turns to the outer world either to help the spouse, the marriage, or the patient, he introduces another frame of reference, which transcends the technique of intrapsychic exploration. Whereas the purpose of the analyst is to help the patient distinguish inner conflicts from reality and, through the transference resolution, to recognize distortions of reality, the analyst who has a relationship with some facet of the patient's reality dilutes his own function of providing inward-directed attention. The introjection of the analytic attitude (the analytic introject) does not occur or does not occur so definitively, and the transference projection of fusion among self-representation, spouse, and analyst becomes intensified. This process takes place because the analyst is actually behaving in a fashion congruent with the patient's fantasies, assuming a role that involves omnipotence and is reminiscent of the early mother-child fusion or symbiosis. By relating to an area of the patient's reality, the analyst is tacitly (or otherwise) promising the patient that he can alter the external world in ways that will significantly help him, that he can produce changes within the patient that do not require self-understanding, internal readjustments, conscious choice, or autonomy.

Transference resolution becomes difficult under these circumstances, for there is a relatively weak formation (cathexis) of the analytic introject and a fairly intense distorted representation of the analyst determined by the transference projection. The ego is therefore impaired in its self-observing function to the extent that the distinction between the analyst and the transference projection is blurred. The patient is unable to view the analyst as analyst but can see him only in terms of an archaic imago. This state results in a transference fixation, which is a hindrance to further analysis. Instead, the patient continues to react to the analyst in terms of his infantile distortions and expectations.

He is also unable to distinguish between his internal *milieu* and the analyst. Because the analyst has become "fused" with the spouse and because this fusion is reinforced by the analyst's relationship with the spouse, the perception of such a relationship is reflected within the ego as a fusion of self- and object representations. An external object relationship inevitably reinforces the mental representation of such a relationship even if the initial intrapsychic formation was created by a projection of infantile attitudes. Under these circumstances, various intra-ego systems become less clearly delineated. The ego becomes less structured and amorphous. This result has therapeutic drawbacks, for the ego cannot achieve an optimal distance from the uncon-

scious and is thereby impaired in its ability to discern conflicting motivations and distortions.

These formulations are conceptual descriptions, and reactions and regressions as intense as those I have described
are not always the rule. I have emphasized the analytic goal
of the resolution of the transference neurosis, which I believe is hampered by introducing an extraneous relationship. The goals of therapy differ, however. I limit myself
here to the analytic process, which sometimes continues in
the direction of resolution even when vicissitudes are introduced. Still, it is best to be aware of the meanings of
parameters in terms consistent with our theoretical understanding.

The study of married couples, insofar as they represent
a particular type of object relationship, has many interesting
implications for the more general developmental aspects of
object relationships. Benedek[21] and Mahler[22] have studied
the early stages of development in adults, using reconstruc-
tive methods, and in children and have postulated an early
stage of fusion between the mother and child, which they
call "symbiosis." Husbands and wives are also bound to each
other in symbiotic fashion. But their bond is of a different
order from that between mother and child. Pollock[23] has
explored the concept of symbiosis thoroughly, and he has
also made the distinction between symbiosis of two adults
and of mother and child. He emphasizes the conclusion that
the symbiotic process can be viewed at different developmental stages. Married couples differ from the mother-child
symbiosis because the needs of one partner for the other
are "equal." The mother may have an intense emotional
need for the child, and the child is, of course, almost totally
dependent upon her. The mother could survive, however,
without the child, whereas the converse is not true. The
study of psychopathology has revealed that one spouse could
not survive psychically if something happened to the marital
relationship. At least, he could not maintain an equilibrium
unless he found someone similar to the lost partner. These
marriages highlight intense mutual dependence. Every mar-

riage, of course, has a degree of mutual dependence inherent in it, one that becomes exaggerated with psychopathology.

Some symbiotic element, therefore, is found in every stable relationship. It is not necessarily the same as that found in early neonatal stages, but it has some resemblance to the initial symbiosis. There are in every object relationship elements of its beginnings, operating even in a contemporary setting. Object relationships reflect their historical development, and, although later derivatives may be the most significant ones, their prototypes still exert some influence.

Early neonatal stages are conceptualized as characterized by a homogeneity between the inner and outer worlds. There is no clear-cut distinction between the self and the outer world. If we can speak of an object relationship at all, we should have to speak of a narcissistic one. Later, however, the external object, by promoting ego structure in general, also contributes to a consolidation of the self-representation. From an initial narcissistic stage, a symbiotic fusion between the mother and child develops through gradual differentiation and separation from the external object, an ego that has its own boundaries. This ego or more precisely the self-representation still contains introjected elements of the initial symbiotic relationship. With further development, these elements become increasingly structured and then differentiated into qualities that determine later object choices.

The early symbiosis is therefore involved in developmental processes and is a factor in such development. Aspects of this symbiosis as they persist in later object choices are highlighted in the study of the psychopathology of the married patient. Early fusion with the mother, although global, nevertheless represents an embryonic self-image. Separation from the mother leads to a consolidation, an individuation, of the self-image and results in a circumscribed identity. Insofar as the projection of the spouse in the transference neurosis reveals a projection of an early self-representation, we can conclude that the symbiotic elements of an object relationship have persisted with considerable intensity. The patient seeks, at one level, elements of the early symbiotic experience in the marital relationship. He attempts to find an early aspect of the self in the spouse.

If the early symbiosis was characterized by destructive elements and the self-representation was a hated and hateful one, then it would block further development. A hostile cathexis of the self impairs ego differentiation and leads to constriction of adaptive techniques. The developmental spectrum of object relationships is also correspondingly narrowed, and, in cases of psychopathology, especially those with characterological defects, the modality for the choice of objects is determined chiefly by the early symbiosis. Mahler's cases of symbiotic children are extreme examples of narrowed object relations determined by symbioses that were felt to be engulfing and destructive.

As a person matures, his capacity to obtain gratification from objects increases. The ego has many adaptive techniques at its disposal, and object relationships have multiple facets enabling the psyche to achieve a wider variety of satisfactions. Both the needs and the techniques of gratification are better developed. One relates to an external object at many different levels. Still, the need to consider an object in terms of one's own self-representation is operative in well developed egos too. The self-representation, however, has many more dimensions than the global fusion in the initial symbiosis. It is a representation that functions in many frames of reference, is well synthesized, and embodies a variety of skills and adjustive techniques. In a well differentiated ego, the self-representation is close to the ego ideal and is highly valued. Similarly, the object is highly valued in the same way as the self. The initial symbiosis has undergone a series of refinements and progressive development leading to an expansive sense of the self that functions smoothly and often creatively. A person seeks a spouse whom he values in the same way that he values himself. The elements of the earlier symbiosis continue to operate even in so-called "mature" object relationships, but they are expansive rather than constrictive because the symbiosis has undergone considerable organization. The person finds that, in order to value another person, he must know how to value himself, and he must rediscover in the other a valued part of the self.

That the psychopathology of the married person is identical or equivalent to that of the spouse is a conclusion based on observation. It is an empirical generalization, and there are exceptions (symptom object relations, for example). The exceptions, however, consist of object relations on a different axis from that of character object relations. They are characterized by superficial involvement and tend to be transient.

Can such an empirical generalization as the equivalence of married partners' psychopathology be integrated into a consistent theoretical framework? If so, an observation that has been explained in terms of a theoretical process becomes more plausible and gains in predictive value, for it is no longer dependent on mere induction. As a construct, the equivalence of psychopathology and even nonpathological character structures as a characteristic of marriage acquires greater validity and conviction than it has when viewed only as a clinical phenomenon.

The projection of the self-representation is often observed as a central feature of the transference neurosis. The analyst can, at different times, be imbued with qualities characteristic of the patient during periods of his past. Sandler[24] and the Hampstead group have noted that, in children too, usually those whose conditions have been diagnosed as borderline states, the projection of archaic aspects of the ego may be the chief transference manifestation. In cases of married adults, different levels of the self-image are projected onto the analyst, depending on the predominant psychosexual orientation of the therapeutic moment.

As we have stressed, whenever the self-representation is projected onto the analyst, regardless of the psychosexual level of the ego state, the analyst is also viewed as a spouse. The analyst, by not behaving in a fashion consistent with such a self representation, enables the patient to correct his distortion and eventually to effect a resolution of the transference neurosis.

Can the spouse also behave in a fashion that is not consistent with the self-representation, while still enabling the patient to maintain this projection? How does the spouse behave if the patient projects an earlier self-representation onto him? Piaget[25] points out that a mental representation (an internal psychic construct) can be maintained in early stages of development only if there is a corresponding external object to reinforce it. Beres[26] makes a similar point about ego regression. In a married couple, it becomes difficult to understand how one spouse can maintain a projection of an infantile self-representation unless it receives some validation from the outside world. Even the paranoid psychotic, who uses projection in an extreme fashion, chooses objects that show some degree of appropriateness for the projection.

If the patient is not able to maintain this type of projection, the marital equilibrium is disturbed. The separation reactions and resistances described occur when one partner is no longer able to project because the other partner is no longer willing to allow it. The latter partner has experienced shifts in his intrapsychic equilibrium that are reflected in changes in his adjustive techniques. Consequently, we can raise the question of what type of psychic organization a person must have in order to behave in a fashion that enables another person to project aspects of an infantile self-representation onto him. If a person is able to behave in a manner congruent with another person's infantile self-representation, it seems inevitable that he has an underlying structure consistent with such behavior. To play a role for a long period of time is difficult, if not impossible, unless the role, to some extent, fits.

The patient's requirements of the spouse are so global and involve so many facets of his behavior that for such a role to "fit" would require specific qualities of the most basic and fundamental aspects of the spouse's psychic structure. The patient's projection includes practically all areas of the spouse's life, domestic and sexual as well as vocational and aesthetic. The evidence for this conclusion again comes from observation of the transference neurosis, for when the analyst is considered as a spouse-self-representation, the patient's associations and fantasies delve into all areas of the analyst's life. Whatever conflictual elements are predominant determine what areas the patient will focus upon. Eventually, with psychodynamic shifts, he covers the gamut of the analyst's personal life, indicating that his need to see the spouse as a certain type of person includes the broader aspects of her personality. In contrast, a person whose marriage is founded on the basis of a symptom object relationship shows a more limited involvement in the broader aspects of the analyst's personal life when the transference of the spouse is the essence of the transference neurosis. In other transference states, in which the spouse is only minimally involved, if at all, the patient's fantasies about the analyst may include many areas.

To recapitulate, because the spouse can behave appropriately relative to the patient's projection of an infantile self-representation, it becomes apparent that the spouse's and the patient's self-representations must be similar. We can then conclude that there has to be an equivalence of psychopathology and a similarity of character structure.

In order to understand how similar self-representations indicate equivalence of psychopathology, we must examine the concept of the self-representation further. The patient reveals that he not only projects a subjective appraisal of an earlier self-image, but he also includes both conflictual and defensive aspects in the transference projection. We note the projection of an ego state that contains conscious and unconscious elements, psychodynamic and characterological features. Psychopathology is the outcome of disturbances of an early self-representation. Psychodynamic conflicts and character defects in the adult can be traced back to and are, in large measure, caused by disturbed early object relations, which in turn contribute to the structure of the self-representation. The last then determines how he adjusts and the quality of his future object relations. Adjustive techniques, defensive or otherwise, are the essence of a person's individuality; the nidus of character structure is already formed in the early self-representation. When we think in terms of similar or identical self-representations, it is therefore conceptually consistent to conclude that the personalities of those compared are similar from all points of view, psychodynamic, characterological, and psychopathological.

Summary

To explore the classical psychoanalytic approach as applied to the treatment of marital disharmony, we must understand precisely what is meant by "classical psychoanalysis." Deviations from so-called "classical" techniques are meaningful only if their implications can be discussed within a consistent theoretical framework. The theoretical scaffolding both of psychoanalytic treatment and of parameters requires elaboration and refinement.

The study of object relations, of which marital partnerships are one type, affords us a good opportunity for such a theoretical study. The frame of reference of the transference neurosis, along with the separation reactions of one partner when the marital equilibrium is disturbed, enables us to conclude that a marriage that has endured is characterized by an equivalence of psychopathology of the spouses.

Introduction of parameters causes complications for transference resolution. The projection of the spouse, at a crucial transference stage, involves a projection of an infantile self-representation; this projection is characterized by the psychic mechanism of fusion of the spouse and the analyst. This spouse-analyst fusion is reinforced if the analyst has an actual relationship with the spouse, which makes resolution difficult.

Symbiosis, a term that has been restricted to an early mother-child fusion, exists at later developmental levels too. We can scrutinize the symbiotic process as a serial hierarchy, a continuum that extends from neonatal stages to adult object relations, including marriage. There are symbiotic elements in both nonpathological and pathological relations, and in both instances they determine the quality of the relationship.

Symbiotic fusion is crucial in the early formation of the self-representation, which can be conceptualized in terms of psychodynamic and characterological elements. The partner, as a recipient of the projection of an infantile self-representation, behaves in a fashion that permits the maintenance of such a projection. The partner is able to behave "appropriately" because he has a similar self-representation. To the extent that an infantile self-representation contains the seeds of later psychopathology and determines nondefensive adjustments, similar or identical self-representations indicate similarity of character structure from both pathological and nonpathological points of view.

NOTES

1. Kurt Eissler, "The Effect of the Structuring of the Ego on Psychoanalytic Techniques," *Journal of the American Psychoanalytic Association,* 1 (1953), 1.

2. Sigmund Freud, "The Dynamics of Transference," *The Standard Edition of the Complete Psychological Works of Sigmund Freud,* 12 (London: Hogarth Press, 1958), 97-107; and Freud, "Remembering, Repeating and Working Through (1914)," *Standard Edition,* 12 (London: Hogarth Press, 1958), 145-57.

3. Ernest Jones, *The Life and Work of Sigmund Freud,* I (New York: Basic Books, Inc., 1953).

4. S. Ferenczi and O. Rank, *The Development of Psychoanalysis* (Nervous and Mental Disease ed.; Baltimore: The Williams & Wilkins Co., 1924).

5. Freud and Joseph Breuer, *Studies on Hysteria* (1895), Standard Edition, Vol. II (London: Hogarth Press, 1958)

6. Clarence P. Oberndorf, "Psychoanalysis of Married Couples," *Psychoanalytic Review,* 25 (1938), 453.

7. Bela Mittlemann, "Complementary Neurotic Reactions in Intimate Relationships," *Psychoanalytic Quarterly,* 13 (1944), 479.

8. Peter L. Giovacchini, "Mutual Adaptation in Various Object Relationships," *International Journal of Psychoanalysis,* 34 (1958), 1-8.

9. A. DeBary, *Die Erscheinung der Symbiose* (Strasbourg: Trubner, 1879).

10. Therese Benedek, "The Psychosomatic Implications of the Primary Unit: Mother-Child," *American Journal of Orthopsychiatry*, 19 (1949), 642; and Benedek, "Parenthood as a Developmental Phase," *Journal of the American Psychoanalytical Association*, 7 (1959), 3.

11. Margaret Mahler, "On Child Psychosis and Schizophrenia: Autistic and Symbiotic Infantile Psychoses," *The Psychoanalytic Study of the Child*, 7 (New York: International Universities Press, Inc., 1952).

12. Edith Jacobson, "The Self and the Object World," *Psychoanalytic Study of the Child*, 9 (New York: International Universities Press, Inc., 1954).

13. Erik H. Erikson: *Identity of the Life Cycle* (New York: International Universities Press, 1959).

14. Anna Freud, "Aggression in Relation to Emotional Development," *Psychoanalytic Study of the Child*, 3-4, (New York: International Universities Press, Inc., 1949), pp. 37-47.

15. Heinz Hartmann, "The Mutual Influences in the Development of the Ego and Id," *Psychoanalytic Study of the Child*, 2, (New York: International Universities Press, Inc., 1946).

16. Ernest Kris, "Notes on the Development and on Some Current Problems of Psychoanalytic Child Psychology," *Psychoanalytic Study of the Child*, 5 (New York: International Universities Press, Inc., 1950).

17. Giovacchini, "Resistance and External Object Relations," *International Journal of Psychoanalysis*, 42 (1961), 246-54.

18. B. Boyer, "Psychoanalytic Treatment of Schizophrenia," *International Journal of Psychoanalysis*, 43 (1961), 389-404.

19. S. Weiss, "Parameters in Child Analysis," paper presented at the fall meeting of the American Psychoanalytic Association, New York City, 1963.

20. E. J. Anthony, "Panel on Child Analysis at Different Developmental Stages," *Journal of the American Psychoanalytic Association*, 12 (1964), 1.

21. Benedek, "Psychosomatic Implications"; and Benedek, "Parenthood."

22. Mahler, *op. cit.*

23. George H. Pollock, "On Symbiosis and Symbiotic Neurosis," *International Journal of Psychoanalysis*, 45 (1964), 1-31.

24. Joseph Sandler and Bernard Rosenblatt, "The Concept of the Representational World," *Psychoanalytic Study of the Child*, 17 (New York: International Universities Press, 1962).

25. Jean Piaget, *Play, Dreams and Imitation* (New York: W. W. Norton and Company, Inc., 1951).

26. David Beres, "Psychoanalytic Psychology of Imagination," *Journal of the American Psychoanalytic Association*, 8 (1960), 252-69.

5

TREATMENT OF
MARITAL DISHARMONY
BY COLLABORATIVE THERAPY

Peter A. Martin

Doctor Martin is an outstanding clinician and teacher from Detroit, Michigan. He and his colleague Doctor H. Waldo Bird have espoused the collaborative treatment of marital problems, which they call the "stereoscopic technique." It is an important method of treatment for marital discord. Doctor Martin has found that in the therapeutic process the therapist's countertransference occupies a position of significance second to no other component, including the patient's transference. To date he has studied fifty couples by this method.

In their classification of current psychotherapeutic approaches to marital disharmony in America, Greene, Solomon, and Lustig[1] define the collaborative technique. They describe it as one in which "each partner was treated by different therapists who communicated for the purpose of maintaining the marriage." Dr. H. Waldo Bird and I were pioneers in the development of the collaborative approach in 1948 and in first reporting on our formalized approach (called the "stereoscopic technique") in 1952.[2] I shall describe our technique at length later in this chapter. At this point, I shall offer another definition of the collaborative approach. As it developed in our experience, the marriage partners were treated by different psychiatrists, who communicated for the purpose of facilitating therapeutic changes in their patients. Therapeutic change was the emphasis and motivating force in the development of our collaborative approach.

Dr. Greene, *et al.*, stress in their definitive paper that the current variety and number (six) of types of technique for treating marital disharmony indicate a great need for flexibility, so that the specific approach can be tailored to the unique marital pattern as well as to the individual needs of the couple. This attitude is ideal for approaching marital disharmony. It presupposes a working knowledge of the six approaches described in this book. Heretofore, each therapist has usually treated marital problems with the one or two approaches with which he was familiar. Utilization of this book thus allows for the development of greater flexibility and variety in the therapeutic armamentarium.

In marked contrast to this sophisticated attitude, our collaborative technique developed spontaneously out of necessity rather than from prior knowledge or any preconceived plan.

The psychiatrist who treats a married person encounters a problem not present in treating an unmarried person, for the intensity of the marriage relationship makes it a fertile field for the development of neurotic conflicts. Emotional upheavals over such conflicts frequently consume large portions of the psychotherapeutic hours. No matter how honest the patient may attempt to be in the treatment situation, the material presented often contains distortions of both his own and his mate's activities and attitudes. Such distortions may be the result of conscious or unconscious defensive efforts.[3] It becomes the task of the psychiatrist to evaluate accurately the disturbed marriage relationship, despite his patient's distortions and omissions of fact.

It often happens that both marriage partners are in therapy simultaneously with different psychiatrists. Each therapist is then faced with the identical task of appraising the true nature of the marital relationship through the screen of his patient's distortions. Under such circumstances, if the two psychiatrists meet, they may discuss the current problems of the marriage partners. Dr. Bird and I developed such occasional discussions into a program of regularly scheduled meetings as an approach to the therapy of marriage partners. It was only after the program had been in operation for some time, however, that we recognized it as a valuable psychotherapeutic tool. One of the psychiatrists had encountered a recurring obstacle to therapeutic success with married persons. Good therapeutic results could often not be achieved because of serious emotional problems in the patient's mate. Such situations necessitated referral to the other therapist, and the practice began with four couples. Through the ensuing years, approximately fifty couples have been studied by this method. Psychoanalytically oriented psychotherapy was utilized. The patients were seen between one and three times a week. These patients were mainly business and professional people in the middle-income brackets with high-school or college backgrounds. None of the original patients entered treatment with marital difficulties as a presenting symptom. The outstanding complaints in the four spouses who first came for treatment were, respectively, attempted suicide, severe depression with anxiety, obsessive-compulsive thoughts and behavior, and agoraphobia. The second set of patients did not begin therapy because they recognized any personal needs but because of pressure from their partners already in treatment. They did not present neurotic complaints that troubled them personally, although some were as sick as their mates. From this description, it can be seen that the authors were dealing with seriously disturbed marriage partners and not with the comparatively simple problems of marriage counseling.[4]

After these referrals, some interesting phenomena occurred. Whenever the psychiatrists met, they *of necessity* compared notes on the therapeutic problems of these couples. These conferences were held not only with the full knowledge and consent of the partners but often also at the insistence of particular partners who requested all possible help with domestic emergencies that had arisen. The term "of necessity" is used to emphasize the stormy courses the therapies followed. These patients were at times so disturbed that such emergency problems as possible suicide, homicide, and desertion, beside actual family brawls, arose and required management.

These at first casual meetings between the two psychiatrists thus became planned meetings. At each meeting, one of the psychiatrists would present a picture of some event that had taken place in the lives of one of the couples. He would present the picture as he had been able to reconstruct it from his patient's productions. His reconstruction was based on a dynamic understanding of his patient and did not therefore represent acceptance at face value of the patient's productions. The other psychiatrist would then report on the same incident as he had reconstructed it from his patient's presentation. A reconstructed picture of some important event as presented by one patient could thus be placed next to the reconstructed picture of the same event as presented by the spouse. This similarity to the principle of a stereopticon led to adoption of the term "stereoscopic technique."

It sometimes happened that these simultaneous views were so out of focus that justifiable doubts were raised about either one patient's veracity or the powers of observation of his psychiatrist. Despite efforts to the contrary, the psychiatrists usually tended to accept as realistic the productions of their own patients more often than was warranted. At times, after one of the psychiatrists had related his reconstruction of an event, he was often shocked into recognition that he had accepted as reality a distortion of reality by his patient. This sudden recognition resulted from having his picture placed alongside that of his colleague. The simultaneous viewing of these two pictures offered the opportunity to recognize the reality distortions. It is this ability to highlight distortions of reality that is the outstanding feature of the stereoscopic technique. This technique helps the psychiatrist to recognize more quickly and more adequately his patient's distortions of reality and thus aids him in his task of confronting the patient with reality. Neurotic, as well as psychotic, patients often have ego defects in reality testing.

As Grotjahn[5] has commented, in writing about our technique, it is not that reality itself is so important. The distortions of reality that we perceive so clearly through our technique are valuable mainly in the development of insights into the interaction between the unconsciouses of two people. As I shall show, it is the underlying neurotic interlock that we wish to uncover as the primary cause of the marital disharmony.

It is advantageous at this point to present clinical material in illustration of the technique's operation. It also describes the neuroses existing in the marriage partners, their treatment, and the influence of countertransference on the process of therapy.

These clinical data have been extracted from the concurrent therapies of a middle-aged husband and wife, both of whom suffered from severe psychiatric disorders. Work with this couple began after the family physician recognized that it would become necessary to hospitalize the wife if psychotherapy were not promptly undertaken. As he was unable to persuade her to seek help, he advised her husband to consult a psychiatrist first, in the hope that she would later follow suit. This device was successful, and the wife usurped her husband's fourth appointment. During her third hour, she insisted that she remain in treatment with the first psychiatrist and that her husband be referred to the colleague.

During the early phase of the wife's treatment, she did little more than criticize her spouse. She complained that he did not love her, that he treated her as his social inferior, and that he wanted to be free of her. She accused him of using alcohol to excess, of neglecting his business, and of failing to discharge his responsibilities as a father. Finally, she condemned him because he had had an affair with his secretary and because he was impotent with her. In this connection, she reported that her husband had once encouraged her to have intercourse with a mutual friend in their own home. She placed little emphasis on her own emotional problems, which she summarized as a tendency to be "inadequate" when forced by the husband's defections to assume unwarranted responsibilities.

The husband made no protest at being referred to a

second psychiatrist. He quietly accepted the blame that the wife heaped upon him, admitting that he had neglected his family and business, that he drank excessively, and that he was impotent with her. He denied, however, her charges that he did not love her, that he wanted to be free of her, and that he had urged her to have an extramarital affair. He said that he wanted to co-operate fully with the therapist and to find out what in his childhood had caused his present difficulties. The opening hours of his treatment were filled with fantasies about an idyllic love relationship with his wife, free of strife and also of physical contact.

In one of the initial conferences between the two psychiatrists, the wife's therapist presented his reconstructed version of the incident in which she had had intercourse with a close friend, allegedly at her husband's instigation. This occurrence was offered as evidence of his rejecting attitude toward her and his inability to act the role of a man. The husband's psychiatrist reacted with skepticism and with sympathy for his patient. He expressed the opinion that the husband had been cuckolded, in view of the fact that the husband had become enraged when he first heard about the incident and had retaliated by revealing to his wife for the first time the earlier affair with his secretary. On this occasion, the stereoscopic technique not only demonstrated its usefulness in detecting a distortion of reality—the falseness of the wife's accusation—but also brought to light what was later recognized as positive countertransference reactions to their respective patients on the part of both psychiatrists. In attempting to understand this distortion and others of equal importance contained in the productions of both marital partners, the therapists became aware of the necessity to investigate further with each patient the defense mechanisms and underlying instinctual impulses involved.

During the next phase of the wife's treatment, the complaint that her husband did not love her recurred constantly. She made only passing references to her own drinking bouts and outbursts of rage and to her inadequacy in domestic and social situations. As memories of her childhood emerged, it became evident that her early life experiences had been characterized by intense fear of being alone and by an exaggerated need to depend on the adults in her home. As a terrified little girl, she had insisted on sleeping on a cot in the dining room, where she would listen intently to family conversations in the adjoining parlor. When finally she was unable to tolerate her loneliness any longer, she would cry out and thus bring her father to her side. She then customarily demanded that he carry her tenderly upstairs. It was as the result of a long series of demands, similarly expressed and met, that she came to be known in her family as the "pink goddess."

An incident of fascinating interest and significance took place during this phase of the wife's therapy. Late one afternoon, the husband urgently summoned her psychiatrist to their home, where the wife was found to be completely inebriated, disheveled, and furious with her husband, who fled the scene as soon as he had admitted the physician to the house. The wife thereupon delivered an hour-long tirade against her spouse, berating him again and again for the affair with his secretary some ten years earlier. The patient's attitude was so violent that the physician too became frightened. Note should be made of the fact that the wife was in the midst of making preparations for her daughter's forthcoming marriage at that time.

During this phase of the husband's therapy, he continued to take full blame for his wife's problems and to protest that he loved her. Psychodynamically relevant material brought into focus a poignant picture of his childhood. As a boy, he had been saddled with the responsibility for the care of a mentally defective younger brother. Their mother had refused to act on recommendations that this boy be institutionalized. The patient was both terrified and humiliated by his brother's violent outbursts and frequent episodes of soiling. One day he forgot to bring his brother home from school for lunch. When he returned for him, he found the school locked but managed to break in to reach his brother. For this action, he was severely reprimanded by both his parents and the school authorities.

In the stereoscopic meetings dealing with the foregoing material, the wife's psychiatrist presented his reconstructed version of the episode of rage that he had witnessed in the patient's home. He concluded that her anger represented intense jealousy of her daughter, who, in the first place, was now the center of the family's attention and whose marriage, in addition, promised to provide her daughter with the love that the patient felt unrealistically she was not receiving from her husband. The colleague's version was somewhat different. He postulated that such rages were not uncommon and that they recurred as often as several times a week. He also concluded that the wife was not acknowledging her spouse's constant protection and his acceptance of her uncontrollable outbursts.

Work with the couple had by that time reached the point at which it was possible to identify each patient's defense system. It was clear that the husband's defense against his own intense hostility toward his brother and mother was a reaction formation in which he became a "good boy" whose ideal was the virtuous, long-suffering, tragic saint. This facade also protected him against fear of castration by his mother and provided satisfaction of his great need to be loved. The defense had, however, begun to crack in recent years, as indicated by the passive expressions of hostility manifested in his impotence, his alcoholism, and his periods of absence from home and from his work. The wife defended herself against hostile impulses and the dependent strivings of a clinging, controlling nature by maintaining her infantile wish to be omnipotent, expressed as a demand that she be treated as a "goddess." This defense mechanism was first threatened by the birth of her oldest child. She was described as having been transiently "psychotic" by the family physician who cared for her at that time. In the intervening seventeen years, the onslaughts of these underlying instinctual impulses had impaired the functioning of her ego to the point where she had become ineffective and inadequate as a wife and mother.

The insights provided by the stereoscopic approach were utilized by the psychiatrists in identifying the pattern of this marriage. The husband's neurosis contained a repetition compulsion in which he recreated with his wife his martyrdom in caring for the uncontrolled idiot brother. His wife's inadequacy, inability to control her violent feelings, and great need for attention certainly strengthened his unconscious identification of her with his brother. The wife was similarly driven by a repetition compulsion, specifically to maintain her infantile wish to be the "pink goddess" who would be loved unconditionally and on demand by her husband, as she had been by her father. Fascinatingly enough, the wife, in her dreams, showed that she had identified herself with the husband's brother. For both partners, the pink goddess and the idiot brother had thus become fused in a single image. As a consequence, an unconscious vicious circle was set in motion, in which the wife's identification with the frightening and demanding idiot forced the husband to adopt the role of an overpassive, martyred "good boy."

We now have come to the point at which we can fully define our approach: The stereoscopic technique, as used in collaborative psychotherapy of marriage partners, consists of planned, regular reviews of two psychiatrists' reconstructed versions of important events in the lives of the partners for the therapeutic purpose of recognizing distortions of reality in the productions of their patients. The therapeutic possibilities of the stereoscopic technique are not limited to this recognition of reality distortions. We found that such recognition led more quickly to recognition of the ego defenses of the patient. Once this important recognition was accomplished, a third important recognition followed: It became possible to recognize the instinctual impulses that were being expressed or warded off.[6]

Even more important, as we became more sophisticated in the use of our technique, a further recognition became possible. We could understand the complementary neuroses that existed between the partners, that both drew them together and pushed them apart. In our example, the wife's representation was that of a baby or idiot child. The husband's neurosis involved self-identification as a martyred, saintly older brother.

We believe that the recognition and exposure of such transference neuroses in the treatment situation are necessary for permanent therapeutic endeavors.

Our approach is in keeping with that of Grotjahn,[7] who states that the mother-child symbiosis is the prototype of the later family, that it is the basis of the child's conscious and unconscious, and that only later will he include the image or ideal of father, brother, sister, grandparents or whomever he meets. Grotjahn argues, "All through our later life we transfer our inner childhood family onto the realistic family and each of us maintains a complicated circular relationship between his parental family, the inner family of his conscious and unconscious, and the projection of these images upon his own family, established when he becomes an adult." He defines the marriage neurosis as the transfer and projection of unresolved, unconscious conflicts from the past of both partners into the present, that is, from childhood families into the marriage situation.

The study of current experiences between the spouses reproduced and made possible for us the reconstruction of even the earliest autistic, symbiotic, or separation phases of infant-mother relationships. Our therapeutic approach is therefore basically psychoanalytically conventional.

With increased sophistication, the stereoscopic technique became an effective instrument, when used judiciously, for treating marital disharmony and has been a welcome addition to our therapeutic armamentorium. Its judicious usage depends, however, upon acute awareness and evaluation of its advantages and disadvantages.

One of the greatest advantages of the stereoscopic technique is its offer of a possibility for ending transference-countertransference duels between different therapists

working with members of the same family. This point can
be illustrated by the following clinical material on the recognition and reduction of negative countertransference reactions.

As the husband's treatment proceeded, he began to
describe the lurid details of his wife's violent bouts of
alcoholism. He related how she criticized him endlessly and
how she often kept him awake all night long, with the result
that he was unable to go to work in the morning. It also
became apparent that, on other occasions, she refused to
allow him to arise, insisting that he remain in bed to cradle
her in his arms. There was, by this time, no doubt in the
psychiatrists' minds that the husband's accounts were authentic and realistic. Yet he maintained that he and he alone
was "at fault," and he accepted as valid even obviously un-
fair accusations by his wife.

In relating this material at the regular meetings of the
psychiatrists, the husband's therapist at first expressed sympathy for a man who was so burdened by a near-psychotic
partner. But, as time wore on and the husband continued
to present the same material in the same manner, his psychiatrist's reports carried a different tone. These later comments implied that it was difficult and unrewarding to work
with such a passive male, a man who continued to be sexually impotent, who rarely went to work on time, and who
drank as much as he ever had. The physician went on to
emphasize that the patient strove mainly to play the role of
the "good little boy" in the treatment hours, while running
away from masculine responsibilities in his daily life.
Because the patient sometimes clowned in the company of
his friends, who then bought him drinks, the psychiatrist
derisively likened him to Little Tommy Tucker, who "sang
for his supper." In further observations, the psychiatrist
stressed the difficulty of inducing the patient to face the
perfectly obvious fact that his activities resulted from fear
of and anger toward his wife. The psychiatrist finally insisted that the prognosis was very poor.

As the wife's psychiatrist listened to his colleague's reports in one of their meetings, it occurred to him to remind his associate that he himself had been frightened by the wife during the visit to the couple's home. After the reality of the wife's violent nature had been re-emphasized in this manner, the question was then raised as to why the husband's therapist had lost sight of this reality. It became apparent almost immediately that his vision had been obscured by strong negative countertransference feelings. When he was thus confronted with his own reaction, he did a bit of self-analysis that forced him to become aware of his own derisive feelings toward a passive male who allowed a woman to run him ragged and who, in this specific instance, was not dealing with the problem of his castration anxiety as the psychiatrist himself had done earlier in his own personal analysis. Once this understanding had been reached by the husband's therapist, a change in the therapeutic *milieu* ensued. It became easier for the psychiatrist to sit patiently through the succeeding hours and to bend his efforts to help the husband with his problem. In the course of time, the patient was able to express openly his repressed hostility toward his wife, and he made progress in working out the castration anxiety excited by her violence. For the purpose of this paper, it suffices to say that the patient thereafter became more openly aggressive and that he regained his potency with his wife.

During this phase of the husband's therapy, the wife's material and behavior continued to be much like that described earlier. As the husband began to assume masculine responsibilities, however, her projections and distortions stood out in bold relief against his more mature activities. For example, the wife reported that her husband, at a birthday party he had arranged in her honor, had attempted to "embarrass" her by being attentive to another woman. The stereoscopic technique revealed that the husband had not favored another woman but that the patient had become so intoxicated as to become a source of embarrassment to all the guests. On another occasion, the patient referred to her husband as being unduly dependent upon her because he had lost his way on a recent motor trip and could not correct his mistake until she had given him explicit directions. The facts were quite different. The husband, an experienced traveler, had made a wrong turn at the insistence of his wife, who had become confused in reading the road map. On still another occasion, immediately following their first successful intercourse in years, she announced her decision to leave her husband. She gave as her reason, "If I were gone, he would not have to be so stubborn and go against my wishes." When the therapist pointed out that it was she who embarrassed her husband, that it was she who was overly dependent, and that it was she who sought to avoid sexual relationships, she retorted that she was being "falsely accused." Almost invariably such denials were followed by overt attempts to gain approval and affection from the doctor. She would protest that she was a pleasant, kind, well-meaning person who did nice things for her family and friends. She recalled, for example, helping a friend's husband select a fur coat for his wife and mowing the lawn in place of her son, who wanted to keep a social engagement.

In the course of the stereoscopic meetings dealing with this material, the wife's psychiatrist at first expressed positive feelings for his patient and stressed her need for understanding and affection. Somewhat later, however, he confided to his colleague that she had proved to be a frustrating patient and that it had become a chore to work with her. In general, his comments took on a note of angry desperation, and he concluded on one occasion by saying that he would go on with the patient because "there just isn't anything else I can do." He reminded the other psychiatrist that the referring physician had called the patient a "pathological liar" and remarked that the term was most appropriate for one who so blithely continued to project and to distort reality. He reported that he had inexplicably cut one of her hours short by ten minutes and had subsequently felt guilty at having deprived a person who so needed love and consideration.

After the husband's therapist had repeatedly heard his colleague place what seemed to be disproportionate emphasis on the wife's "need to be loved," he made two discerning observations. He commented that the wife's psychiatrist not only had "fallen for the pink goddess line" but also was overlooking the fact that the wife needed to become more adequate. This confrontation placed the responsibility squarely on the wife's therapist to investigate and eliminate the blind spots he had developed. His subsequent self-analysis disclosed a negative countertransference attitude toward the wife, which he had until then denied. In reality, the psychiatrist feared and disliked her, a destructive woman, but he had defended himself against these feelings through the device of overevaluating and overprotecting her. As a consequence, he had been led into establishing the same kind of relationship with her as had existed between her and her father, the first person to be controlled by the "pink goddess." It was then evident that, as long as she could maintain her omnipotent defense against the recognition of her inadequacy, hostility, and dependence, no progress could be made.

Once her therapist had dealt with his negative countertransference, his need to support her powerful defense no longer existed. With the lifting of this defense, work with the underlying impulses proceeded. As a result, the wife took some forward steps. She enlarged the scope of her activities and the circle of her friends, came to demand less of her husband, and eventually agreed to dispose of their pretentious and financially burdensome house.

I should now like to discuss general points about countertransference in the light of our experience with the stereoscopic technique. While we had been made aware of the importance of our own countertransference reactions through clinical experience and in the course of our personal analyses, it was merely an awareness of a principle of psychotherapy by which our work was generally guided. When, in the course of using the stereoscopic technique, each therapist was confronted with the inescapable fact that his feelings had erected an obstacle to therapeutic progress by these patients, this general awareness became a conviction that, in the psychotherapeutic process, the therapist's countertransference occupies a position of significance second to no other component, including the patient's transference. This conviction led us to re-emphasize with each other the fact that the therapist's own analysis is interminable, in the sense that the psychotherapist must ceaselessly analyze his own feelings toward every patient under his care.

It has been recognized[8] that the further the therapeutic method deviates from classical psychoanalytic technique, the greater the danger of unfavorable influence from countertransference feelings. The patients under discussion, like too many others, were not candidates for classical psychoanalysis, with its emphasis on uninterrupted free association. As a matter of fact, the stereoscopic approach utilized in such therapies represents a wide deviation from the traditional procedure, in that the therapist actively confronts one partner with conclusions arrived at in joint conference with his colleague. In making these repeated confrontations, the therapist is certainly afforded unexcelled opportunities to express countertransference feelings. Such opportunities, however, do not present themselves only in the stereoscopic approach but recur in any therapy in which the physician is "active." What is characteristic of the stereoscopic technique is its inherent ability to reflect the therapist's countertransference in the mirror of his colleague's observations.

The stereoscopic technique provides a particularly valuable means of breaking through the therapist's resistance to the recognition of his countertransference reaction. Nothing penetrates this resistance so deftly as a comment like, "You have fallen for the pink goddess line." Such an observation is effective when it is made by a colleague with whom the therapist has the kind of warm working relationship essential to the use of this technique. In addition, the stereoscopic approach makes possible the early detection of countertransference reactions, as is also illustrated in the example. This early detection not only results in a saving of effort and time by the patient involved but also considerably reduces the possibility of a severe transference neurosis that might lead to premature termination of the therapy.

Even when the therapist has appraised his countertransference, the problems encountered in establishing the validity of this appraisal are greatly minimized, in our opinion, by use of the stereoscopic technique. This approach not only provides the involved therapist with the more objective point of view of his uninvolved associate but also makes available to him a realistic and accurate evaluation of the conscious attitudes, defenses, and unconscious impulses of his patient, to which he is reacting, often without his conscious knowledge. For instance, in the case material presented, the wife's therapist was consciously responding to her "need to be loved" and reacting unconsciously to the destructive and dependent impulses underlying the "pink goddess" defense.

The most significant development in the therapies of the couple under consideration was the reduction of the negative countertransference reactions and their replacement by positive countertransference feelings. These positive countertransferences facilitated the husband's work with the problem of his castration anxiety and the wife's recognition of her hostile impulses and dependent strivings. It is our belief that use of the stereoscopic technique brought on this chain of events.

A full exposition of the operation of the stereoscopic technique must include a description of its advantages and disadvantages to the therapists. It is advantageous because it frees the psychiatrist from his single observation post. It brings to him an advantage that the general practitioner of medicine enjoys—information on more than one member of a family.[9] It is also analogous to the advantageous position of the psychiatrist who has completed the therapy of one mate and who then undertakes the treatment of the other,[10] and to the position of the psychiatrist who treats married couples concurrently.[11]

Other advantages are first, a saving of time for the patient, which results from quicker recognition of his distortions of reality. The technique may even pick up distortions that might otherwise never be recognized by the psychiatrist.

Second, it offers opportunities for scientific research in private practice. The therapists are in complete agreement with Dunbar, who writes, "It would appear that the psychiatrist in private practice may increase his therapeutic success and add materially to the general fund of medical knowledge if he takes advantage of his assets and trains himself, as an integral part of his therapeutic procedure, to make and record the kind of careful observation required of the research scientist."[12]

Third, an intellectual stimulant is available to the two psychiatrists as is a sound method of continuing psychiatric training through mutual exchange of ideas.

Fourth, a reduction of the anxiety of one or both partners takes place. It was frequently possible to influence one of the patients to give up a piece of neurotic behavior that had been threatening to the mate. For example, a sadistic husband removed a loaded revolver, easily accessible to his frightened and depressed wife, as a result of her request transmitted through her psychiatrist. He would have done so only on the strength of his positive transference to his psychiatrist. He would never have done so at the request of his wife's psychiatrist.

Fifth, this technique has a tendency to be self-eliminating. As the psychiatrist becomes sensitive to distortions repeatedly picked up by the technique, he begins to recognize them on his own. The more skilled the psychiatrist becomes in using this technique, the less he needs it, which is as it should be. Therapeutic effectiveness depends on the therapist and not on any technique.

The disadvantages to the psychiatrists are, first, that it is more time-consuming. Utilization of this team approach demands regular planned conferences between the psychiatrists. As lack of time is a realistic problem, this demand must be considered a disadvantage. When viewed from the point of view of further training, scientific research, and sharpening of therapeutic skills, however, the compensation for this time is great.

Second, the psychiatrist faces an added task of working out a relationship with his colleague. This relationship can be as difficult and as sensitive as those between the doctors and their patients. If the effort is successful, however, the reward of a close, warm, permanent relationship with a colleague is well worth the difficulties that have to be worked through.

Disadvantages to the patient include first, the intrusion of the new physician-physician relationship into the doctor-patient relationship. This intrusion is perhaps the most serious disadvantage to the patient. The natural development of the countertransference is seriously impeded at times by this physician-physician relationship. For example, the psychiatrist who has come to realize in a conference with his colleague that his patient has unwittingly or otherwise duped him may be harsher in revealing this information to the patient than if he had come to recognize it on his own months later. Once this disadvantage is recognized and worked through completely by the psychiatrists, however, it can be turned to the advantage of the patient through the time saving.

Second, change in the availability of one psychiatrist breaks up the therapeutic team and the prearranged use of the technique.

I should like to conclude that, as there are "many ways to skin a cat," many techniques can accomplish the same job. It is the skill of the individual using the technique that determines its degree of efficacy. It is well for the therapist to be as versatile as possible, in order to achieve the ideal of flexibility and specificity in his approach to marital disharmony.

NOTES

1. Bernard L. Greene, Alfred P. Solomon and Noel Lustig, "The Psychotherapies of Marital Disharmony," *Medical Times,* 91 (1963), 243-56.

2. Peter A. Martin and H. Waldo Bird, "An Approach to the Psychotherapy of Marriage Partners—The Stereoscopic Technique" (read at the Annual Meeting of the American Psychiatric Association in Atlantic City, May, 1952), *Psychiatry,* 16 (1953), 123-7.

3. Bela Mittlemann, "Simultaneous Treatment of Both Parents and Their Child," *Samiksa,* 3 (1949), 213-22.

4. Robert W. Laidlaw, "The Psychiatrist as Marriage Counselor," *American Journal of Psychiatry,* 106 (1950), 732-6.

5. Martin Grotjahn, "Analytic Family Therapy," Jules Masserman, ed., *Individual and Familial Dynamics* (New York: Grune & Stratton, Inc., 1958), pp. 90-104.

6. George Gero, "The Concept of Defense," *Psychoanalytic Quarterly,* 20 (1951), 569-70.

7. Grotjahn, *Psychoanalysis and the Family Neurosis* (New York: W. W. Norton and Company, Inc., 1960), pp. 91-2.

8. Bird and Martin, "Countertransference in the Psychotherapy of Marriage Partners," *Psychiatry,* 19 (1956), 353-60.

9. Clarence P. Oberndorf, "New Possibilities in Private Practice," *American Journal of Psychiatry,* 105 (1949), 589-93.

10. Oberndorf, "Psychoanalysis of Married Couples," *Psychoanalytic Review,* 25 (1938), 453.

11. Mittlemann, "The Concurrent Analysis of Married Couples," *Psychoanalytic Quarterly,* 17 (1948), 182.

12. Flanders Dunbar, "Research in Private Practice," *American Journal of Psychiatry,* 107 (1951), 739-42.

6

CONCURRENT PSYCHOANALYTIC THERAPY IN MARITAL DISHARMONY

Alfred P. Solomon and Bernard L. Greene

More than twenty-five years ago, Doctor Clarence P. Oberndorf wrote about the psychoanalysis of married couples. He did not, however, see it as concurrent but as consecutive. The late Doctor Bela Mittlemann was the first to report his analytic experiences with concurrent therapy. Few analysts have ventured to attempt this technique, the great majority being biased by their one-to-one patient orientations. An exception is Doctor Solomon. I am deeply indebted to him for encouraging me in the use of this technique.

This paper is devoted to the technique and rationale of concurrent psychoanalytic therapy, one of the psychotherapies the authors propose for the treatment of marital disharmony. They are currently engaged in a project to determine criteria for the use of this and other techniques being developed for the purpose. In concurrent psychoanalytic therapy, both spouses are treated separately but synchronously by the same therapist. The authors have found this technique to be of value in treating marital discord, when a therapy must deal with intrapsychic material and with family transactions as well. As a technique, it offers additional dimensions for the mobilization of unconscious material, for the production of intellectual and emotional insights, for the timing of mutative interpretations, for "working through" resistance, and for "working out" new patterns of behavior. The material in this report has been drawn from the authors' current collaborative thinking in their continuing clinical investigation, now in its ninth year.[1] During this interval, they have further refined the technique and have observed its value as a therapy and the nature of its therapeutic action. To date, seventy couples have undergone or are undergoing concurrent treatment.

Dr. Bela Mittlemann,[2] a pioneer in the use of analytic concurrent therapy for married couples, and the late Dr. Franz Alexander,[3] whose writings have for many years inspired those experimenting with modifications of psychoanalytic techniques, have been most influential in our theoretical thinking. We differentiate between psychoanalysis, an individually oriented therapy, and concurrent psychoanalytic therapy, which involves triadic transactions.[4]

Indications

The selection of concurrent psychoanalytic therapy as the form of treatment is determined by the couple's clinical need for a therapy in depth, their capacities for self-observation, their tolerance of the tensions of an uncovering therapy, their possibilities for change in ego resources, absence of contraindications, and the availability of a therapist with psychoanalytic orientation and technical ability to apply this knowledge in a flexible manner.

The authors[5] have previously reported their thinking about indications and contraindications for concurrent treatment. For the purposes of clarifying indications, they divided their patients into two groups. The first group included those couples who spontaneously sought help primarily because of marital problems, often because of the threat of impending divorce. In this group were couples who were motivated to continue their marriage because of unconscious neurotic transactions; unconscious fear of melancholic reaction to divorce; important transactional influences related to nuclear and extended families; religious considerations; and economic-social matters. In the second group, concurrent treatment was recommended to the partners of spouses already in individual office or hospital therapy because of clinical indications for the improvement of the marriage relationships or for overcoming therapeutic impasses. Frequently, the unconscious resistance behavior of the spouse in treatment provoked malignant opposition from the other or, paradoxically, evoked emotional support from the other, thus producing feedback transactions that led to therapeutic stagnation. This group also contained spouses who, while not in treatment, became anxious because of fears of alteration in role complementarity and consequently attempted to sabotage the treatment of their partners. Still other spouses undergoing individual treatment were found to be withholding information about their marital behavior because of their unwillingness to share the responsibility for marital disharmony or because of their anxious fears of disrupting neurotic marriage equilibriums.

Contraindications

The contraindications for this form of therapy were determined by our clinical experience. They are subject to modification upon further experimentation and investigation. According to our present thinking, contraindications exist in some patients with severe psychoses or severe character disorders; in patients with paranoid reactions; in patients exhibiting undue suspicious attitudes toward the communications of their spouses; in patients with excessive sibling-rivalry attitudes that preclude sharing the therapist; in patients in whom psychoses or severe psychoneurotic reactions might develop if the homeostatic balance in neurotic marriage transactions were disturbed; in some patients who, in their individual diagnostic interviews, communicate information about episodes of acting out behavior, like infidelity or homosexuality, unknown to the other partner; and in patients who seem persistently to utilize the therapeutic situation to manipulate their spouses.

Basis for an Operational Approach

Our operational approach is based on our concept of the nature of marital disharmony. We consider marital disharmony a symptom complex determined by transactions between spouses, who are, as individuals, embedded in a social matrix—while nevertheless possessing unique intrapsychic structures with individual value systems and aspirations, individual family and cultural backgrounds, and individual conscious or unconscious anticipations of marriage that may or may not have been fulfilled. These symptom complexes result from breakdowns in equilibrium, from either intrapsychic or transactional tensions, and range from situational reactions at one end of the spectrum to neurotic or psychotic patterns at the other. We prefer the use of the more inclusive term "transaction" to that of "interaction" to describe interpersonal relationships in marriage. "Transaction" refers to a reciprocal process that includes a two-phase cyclical exchange that may become homeostatic on multiple psychological and environmental levels. These homeostatic transactions become characteristic of the marriage. We have found the concept of transaction more useful for therapeutic orientation than the familiar one of interaction. Interaction implies the reaction of one person and the response of the other, without feedback reactions, while transaction encompasses a continuing exchange of communication between individuals in a given social field, the constant feedbacks resulting in changes in the subsequent responses of each person in the field. Our idea of the transactional process has been influenced by the work of Spiegel[6] and Grinker.[7] In our theoretical thinking, we have continued to move from consideration of the marital state as a purely psychological model in relation to the individual involved to incorporation not only of intrapsychic factors but also of the concept that persons are experiencing, transacting, learning individuals with interpersonal relationships related to multiple social and cultural influences. The psychodynamics of our operational approach thus consist of a core of psychoanalytic constructs, to which are added cultural, social psychiatric, communications, and learning concepts.

Fundamental to our consideration of the marriage transaction is the well recognized observation that, in addition to the "real" relationships of the husband and wife, there exists, as in all object relationships, a tendency in their contemporary positive, negative, or ambivalent attitudes to *transfer* onto each other their memories of significant infantile and childhood experiences, thus investing real objects with qualities from the past. As our operational approach was developed, we became aware that additional light could be thrown on these concepts by Melanie Klein's conclusions on *projective identification*. She points out that the projective mechanisms of major importance in identification are complementary to the introjective ones. She traces superego development to the introjection of "good" and "bad" concepts from the earliest stages of infancy. "A securely established good object, implying a securely established love for it, gives the ego a feeling of riches and abundance which allows for an outpouring of libido, and a projection of good parts of the self into the external world without a sense of depletion arising . . . the ego can then also feel that it is able to reintroject the love it has given out, as well as take in goodness from other sources, and thus be enriched by the whole process . . . conversely, the breast taken in with hatred, and therefore felt to be destructive becomes the prototype of all bad internal objects, and drives the ego to further splitting . . . Identification by projection implies a combination of splitting off parts of the self and projecting them onto (or rather into) another person."[8] Melanie Klein calls our attention to the fact that the "process which underlies the feeling of identification with other people, was generally taken for granted even before the corresponding concept was incorporated into psychoanalytic theory. For instance the projective mechanism involved in empathy is familiar in everyday life."[9]

Anna Freud[10] describes still another kind of projection onto a loved object and an identification with the projected image in presenting her concept of altruistic surrender. As an example of this surrender of instinctual impulses, she suggests an altruistic attachment of a woman to her husband in her expectation that he will be able to carry out in her place projects that she believes herself unable to do because of her sex, such as living the life of a student, adopting a particular profession, or becoming famous or rich.

Studies of the ego ideal and superego, particularly that of Piers and Singer,[11] have influenced us in elucidating certain projective identifications involving the introjects producing feelings of shame and guilt, with resultant marital disharmonies. Their description of the ego ideal that contains introjected images of the narcissistically overexpectant parents or their surrogates finds unusual application in the understanding of the transactions in many conflicted marriages. Marital disharmony may result when one spouse, possessing such an ego ideal, projects onto his partner or members of his nuclear or extended family, the image of the excessively demanding, critical ego ideal. Under these conditions, the projecting spouse reacts to his partner, the repository of a library of projected introjects, with a constant need for the partner's praise or approval. When these feelings seem to be withheld, fear and rage directed toward the partner ensue. Variations in the clinical manifestations are highly individualized and depend upon the partner's compliance with or rebellion against the perfectionist, overexpectant ego ideal. In the *projective identification,* the spouse seeks in his mate conscious conformity to his own ego ideal standards, which he is inwardly rebelling against and which keep him under constant stress. Relaxation of this conformity by the partner leads to criticism and withdrawal of love by the projecting spouse, who also feels them empathetically himself.

A most important contribution to understanding the significance of the projective identifications in marital tensions was made by Henry Dicks and his coworkers[12] at the Tavistock Clinic of London, England. They pointed out that such identifications are the basis for an *unconscious collusive process* in the marriage transaction. We heartily support his statement that "in marital disharmony one or both partners often fail to confirm the other's personality or identity. Instead they require the other to conform to an inner role mode, and punish them if the expectation is disappointed." He believes that much marital conflict stems from efforts to coerce or mold the partner by very rigid and stereotyped tactics to these inner models, "and although these techniques arouse resistance and frustrations of the other spouse's ego, needs at a deeper level are part of a collusive process." We are in accord with these observations and with his comment that, where projection identifications have taken place, "hate is felt to be both inside the self towards object, and towards the self in the object from the outside."

A vignette from the case history of one of our couples illustrates the nature of the unconscious projective identification, the spouses' transactional responses to these projections, and the unconscious collusive process that results.

Mr. and Mrs. A were referred by their minister, who had become aware during the course of pastoral counseling that a deep-seated marital problem existed and that intensive therapy was needed.

The husband who was twenty-four years older than his wife, had during the ten years of their marriage, persistently attempted to mold his wife into an individual compliant and submissive to his wishes. She, with equal energy and consistency, worked out means to defy his coercive and manipulating attitudes. She refused to perform tasks that he militantly assigned to her, overslept, rejected household responsibilities, ignored his concepts of fashion, and refused to have her expenditures dictated. As he discovered these acts and attitudes of defiance, sometimes overt and sometimes hidden, he made even more aggressive attempts to control her behavior. His resentment was always associated with feelings of self-justification. Later he frequently complained of his wife to their respective parents, blaming her for their marital discord. He steadfastly refused to comply with his wife's wishes that he ignore his mother's frequent demands for attention and visits. He refrained from giving her any information about his business affairs, despite her insistence, and rejected as criticism any comments she might make on assumptions from other sources. These acts further enraged his wife, who responded by continuing her acts of defiance and by frequent upbraiding but made no attempt to leave her husband. Instead, she met with anxiety any overt suggestion that he might leave her.

In her sex life, Mrs. A was seductive, and both spouses reported reciprocal pleasure. Invariably, however, following their sexual experiences she would heap recriminations upon him about his general inadequacies as a husband.

Significantly, Mrs. A, prior to her marriage, exhibited toward her parents hostile acts similar to those she displayed toward her husband. There, too, she left clues so that her acts of defiance could easily be discovered. Discovery would lead to repetitive efforts on their part to control her behavior. Whenever possible, Mrs. A's mother nagged her husband into attempting to discipline their daughter. Mrs. A reacted with rage, abuse, self-justification, and rationalizations that her mother was attempting to sabotage her good relationship with her father. She became very adroit in her devices to alienate her father's affection from her mother, often secretly persuading her father to concede that her mother had been unjust and unduly critical of her behavior. Her mother, alert to these manipulative machinations, fought back aggressively. Under these conditions, Mrs. A would eventually confess and promise to make amends, and a period of peace would ensue.

From early childhood on, it was apparent that her father was very close to her, engaging in acts of kindness, interest, and affection in the presence of opposition, overt jealousy, and recrimination from her mother. Although Mrs. A had some memories of a kind and giving mother in the psychiatrist's presence, her mood was one of condemnation. She displayed overt hostility in the presence of guilt feelings, related to thinly disguised death wishes. Her regressive, dependent needs led to provocative acting out of her wishes to be watched over and, ambivalently, to her rebellion against these infantile needs.

Mr. A's attachment to his mother, who had continually

from his childhood on demanded high standards of achievement from him, was manifested in his excessive need to please her. This attitude included exaggerated compliance with her hypochondriacal demands for service and attention. Although Mr. A's visits to his mother were largely motivated by his wish to be considered the "good son," they also provided occasions on which he could talk over with her his business and family affairs. Mr. A's relatives and he himself regarded his mother as a person totally dependent on him, although Mrs. A believed that the reverse was true and that her mother-in-law utilized her possessive dependence as a means of controlling him. Mr. A in his business dealings and in relationships with members of his family other than his mother was an aggressive, dominant, willful, and clever man. He expressed contempt for weakness, inefficiency, inaccuracy, and impracticality—behavior typical of his father.

In the psychodynamic formulation of this couple's marriage neurosis, we observed that the projective identifications of Mrs. A were derived from early introjects with her parents. Although there were clinically fleeting evidences of a good mother image, this image had been largely dulled by a multitude of maternal introjects of a hostile, depriving, rejecting, unempathetic, controlling person, whom she had never learned to trust. Prominent in her self-representation were her own identifications with an image of a mother consistently and cleverly trying to undermine the affection between herself and her father.

The good images of the father were identifications with the introjects of the paternalistic, feeding, rearing, and affectionate parent, which found expression in her own tendencies to be giving, trusting, and kind. Bad images of her father were those of the primitive, censorious father, elaborated by identifying him as a person who, at her mother's insistence, co-operated with her. At a conscious level, Mrs. A tried to see her father as good and her mother as bad.

In her marriage, Mrs. A projected this library of good and bad introjects of her parents onto her husband. Mr. A,

because of his personality development, fitted her unconscious morbid needs unusually well. A wish to fulfill these
needs was a positive factor in her choice of a mate. At a
conscious level, she reacted with defiance to his punitive
restrictions and directions, just as she had originally reacted
to those of her mother. Simultaneously, she felt unconscious
hostility arising from these ambivalent introjected and projectively identified images. She aggressively attempted to
undermine the affection between her husband and her
mother-in-law, who was also projectively identified with the
"part" of her alienating mother, as she had earlier attempted
to alienate her parents from each other. Her husband's
angry refusal to comply with her wishes led to his persistence
in his attentions to his mother and an increase in his wife's
feelings of frustration, anger, and regressive fear of aban-
donment. In her marital sexual experiences, masochistically
toned, she gained feelings of triumph, but they were short-
lived.

Mrs. A's collusive attachment to her husband was based
on the unconscious hope, an aspiration in her courtship,
that some day she could mold her husband into a person
who would give up his mother. This hope, however, was
destined never to be fulfilled because of unconscious ambivalence and guilt feelings. These guilt feelings, which led to
her masochistic tolerance of her husband's attitudes, added,
in spite of her vigorous protests, a cementing force to their
collusive marriage transaction.

Mr. A had multiple introjected images of his mother
and father. Important for our consideration of his projective
identifications and the nature of the collusive process were
his images of his mother. His good image was that of the
feeding, loving, rearing mother, who regarded him as the
good son "who could do no wrong" and who rewarded him
with love for behavior that pleased her. Closely associated
with this good image was a bad image, in which he identified her as one who withdrew love when he did not comply
with her standards of performance. Furthermore, he was
unconsciously enraged at his mother for frustrating his un-

conscious dependent needs. His reactions to the hypochondriacal aspects of her demands for conformity with her
wishes were feelings of helpless compliance, motivated by
fear of withdrawal of her love associated with deep-seated
unconscious fear of retaliation for primitive rage against the
infantile incorporated images of the bad mother.

Mr. A's choice of a wife was largely motivated by this
fear of helplessness and its elaboration. As he made sacrifices
to support his mother's rationalizations that she was an
invalid, he sought as a defense a bride whom he could control yet who would resist this control. In his marriage, he
projected onto his wife the standards and controlling pressures of his ego ideal, attempting to mold her into a woman
who would comply with his standards of performance—the
standards of his overexpectant mother. He also projectively
identified, collusively, the part of himself that was in rebellion, secretly promoting rebellion against his own demands, rebellion he dared not exhibit toward his mother
or toward his introjected image of her. Reinforcement of
such unconscious collusion was found in the projective
identification of his father, as an inadequate, irresponsible
person, onto his wife, whom he then hostilely criticized.
Further reinforcement of the collusive contract was found
in his projection onto Mrs. A of his introject of his mother,
upon whom he was dependent and whom he had to control.
We thus see on the unconscious level the collusive, reciprocal elements of the complementary satisfaction of unrecognized needs.

Therapeutic Elements and Therapeutic Action

Concurrent therapy as a technique contains specific
therapeutic elements and a therapeutic action inherent in
its design and operational approach. A couple that is under
great stress reacts to acceptance for concurrent therapy with
feelings that they are getting emotional support. Patients
react to acceptance and emotional support as potent thera-

peutic agents for the relief of their anxiety. We are reminded here of the late Franz Alexander's[13] comment that the supportive effects of the psychoanalytic process have not been sufficiently recognized as one of the main factors favoring both insight and the emergence of new emotional patterns.

There is another important therapeutic gain in a technical procedure that extends hope for the restoration of equilibrium in a marital relationship. When they have hope, the couple co-operates more readily in the painful experience of examining unconscious, unattainable hopes that have led to the marriage crisis and in the substitution of new, conscious, and attainable goals and hopes. Thomas M. French[14] has repeatedly emphasized hope as an integrative force. As in all psychotherapy, suggestion is again an important therapeutic element.

Another therapeutic element in concurrent psychoanalytic therapy is the multidimensional view of the marriage transaction gained by the psychiatrist from the communications of the spouses in a frame of reference often contradictory and constantly changing. These feelings and reports are communicated both explicitly and implicitly in the partners' behavior, in their accounts of situations involving each other, in their descriptions of their attitudes toward each other, in their dreams, and in their transference transactions. Through this *triadic communication system,* knowledge is gained, in minimal time, of both the nuclear and extended family transactions and of the immediate and peripheral environmental situations and influences. The analyst hears both sides of long-standing controversies, and each patient is aware that he is hearing about them from the other spouse also. This latter therapeutic effect is made possible by patients agreeing, as a characteristic of the therapy, not to discuss with their spouses the selective contents of their respective interviews. It has been our clinical experience, however, that, as the concurrent therapy proceeds, some partners do discuss between themselves ideas gained through emotional and intellectual insights. Particularly in the later phases of the therapy, this type of communication may become an extension of the learning process. On the other hand, these incidents often reveal to the therapist additional information about his patients' resistances or about the significance of the resentments, frustrations, or projections produced by these interspouse communications. The communication of unconscious sibling-rivalry attitudes or oedipal feelings, as highlighted in the triangular representation of the original family constellation, is a further therapeutic element.

We direct our patients to report their dreams because we find that dream material enables us to grasp important preoccupations behind the behavioral facades. This knowledge aids us in planning meaningful therapeutic maneuvers for personal affective needs. Further, dreams furnish us with many important clues about the patients' ego integrative problem-solving functions and bring freely into focus the precise nature of introjective and projective identifications and their feedbacks.

Another distinctive therapeutic element in concurrent therapy is the triangular transference. We have described this element in a previous communication,[15] in which we differentiated five foci of transactions in the transference relationships. We stated that the first focus of transaction involves *"the relationship to the therapist as a real person* and subsequently, as a *new object* as well. The second focus of transaction pertains to those situations where the analyst is experienced as a *symbolic figure* endowed with qualities of *existing fantasies,* as those involved in projections and displacements. The regressive phenomena manifested *in the dyadic,* one-to-one, *transference neurosis* comprise the third focus of transaction. These three foci are fundamental in all transference relationships. In concurrent psychoanalytic therapy, because *the transference reactions of both spouses are directed toward the same therapist as well as toward each other,* two other foci of transaction related to the *triangular transference transactions* are introduced. *The first of these is the triangular transference neurosis,* such as the reproduction of the Oedipal constellation. The second, *the triangular transference transactions concern the production* of adaptive feedbacks not only toward the analyst, but also to the other spouse who in turn feeds back to his spouse, to the analyst, or to both." Light is thrown on the nature of these feedbacks by the introjective and projective identification mechanisms that also appear in transference dreams. Interpretations of the transference in concurrent therapy are made when indicated from the frame of reference of *both* the dyadic and the triangular aspects of the transference.

The additional foci of transaction favor the increased production of emotional and intellectual insights, which is conducive to the learning process. The late Franz Alexander[16] recently described the nature of the therapeutic learning process. He wrote, "during treatment the patient unlearns the old patterns and learns new ones. . . . This process . . . . contains cognitive elements as well as learning from interpersonal experiences, which occur in therapeutic interaction." He compares emotional insight to any intellectual grasp "motivated by some kind of urge for mastery and is accompanied by tension resolution as its reward. In psychotherapy the reward consists in less conflictual, more harmonious interpersonal relations, which the patient achieves first by adequately relating to his therapist, then to his environment, and eventually to his own ego ideal."

A summary of a clinical case report of a couple treated with concurrent psychoanalytic therapy has previously been reported in the literature.[17]

Conclusions

This paper has been designed to present the rationale and technique of concurrent psychoanalytic therapy. It has been the experience of both authors that this technique has distinctive therapeutic advantages. It makes possible an analysis of the dyadic, one-to-one transference neurosis and an analysis of the resistance of a patient who knows that another member of his family is being treated synchronously by the same psychiatrist. It brings under focus a more comprehensive view of family transactions, in both the dyadic and triadic transference relationships. The analyst is thus able to achieve a multidimensional view of marital transactions and disharmony and, with this view, a better comprehensive basis for marital psychodiagnosis and treatment. This technique finds selective use for couples who require understanding of intrapsychic processes as they are reflected in and become part of the marital transactions. Indications and contraindications for selecting this therapy have been given. Furthermore, the authors have found that working with this technique has significantly expanded their understanding of family transactions.

NOTES

1. Bernard L. Greene, "Marital Disharmony: Concurrent Analysis of Husband and Wife. I. Preliminary Report," *Diseases of the Nervous System,* 21 (February, 1960), 1-6; Alfred P. Solomon and Greene, "Marital Disharmony: Concurrent Analysis of Husband and Wife by the Same Psychiatrist. III. An Analysis of the Therapeutic Elements and Action," *Diseases of the Nervous System,* 24 (January, 1963), 105-13; and Greene and Solomon, "Marital Disharmony: Concurrent Psychoanalytic Therapy of Husband and Wife by the Same Psychiatrist. IV. The Triangular Transference Transactions," *American Journal of Psychotherapy,* 17 (July, 1963), 443-56.

2. Bela Mittlemann, "The Concurrent Analysis of Married Couples," *Psychoanalytic Quarterly,* 17 (1948), 182-97.

3. The selected papers of Franz Alexander, in *The Scope of Psychoanalysis, 1921-1961* (New York: Basic Books, Inc., 1961), permits the reader to follow closely as he incorporates new parameters of scientific discovery into his psychoanalytic system.

4. John Frosch and Nathaniel Ross, eds., *The Annual Survey of Psychoanalysis,* V (New York: International Universities Press, Inc., 1954), 302, cite Edward Glover, who gives, in "The Indications for Psychoanalysis," *Journal of Mental Science,* 100, 303-401, a working definition of psychoanalytic therapy "in terms of certain fundamental concepts. These are the existence of the unconscious; infantile sexuality; repression; unconscious conflict; and transference. He also feels that whoever holds these fundamental concepts, understands the processes of mental development by which they are arrived at; has taken steps by personal analysis to eliminate as far as possible, the

errors of subjective biases; has learned to apply the technique of association and interpretation; and is capable of analyzing, as far as possible, the transferences and countertransferences that arise in the analytic situation—that this person can call his treatment psychoanalytic therapy. Of these conditions, the capacity and determination to analyze the transference is decisive when drawing a distinction between psychoanalysis and other forms of psychotherapy." Sigmund Freud, in "On the History of the Psychoanalytic Movement," *Collected Papers,* I (London: Hogarth Press, 1924), 298, defined psychoanalysis as a therapy utilizing the principles of transference, resistance, and the concept of unconscious mental activity. He specifically stated, "Any line of investigation, no matter what its direction, which recognizes these two facts (transference and resistance) and takes them as the starting point of its work may call itself psychoanalysis, though it arrives at results other than my own." In the introduction to *Psychoanalytic Therapy,* Alexander, in Alexander and Thomas M. French, eds. (New York: Ronald Press Company, 1946), p. vii, states, "French was the first among us to state explicitly that there is no essential difference between the various procedures, that the differences lie merely in the extent to which the various therapeutic principles are utilized." Freud himself frequently modified his hypotheses, and in his last work, *An Outline of Psychoanalysis* (New York: W. W. Norton and Company, Inc., 1949), p. 36, stated, "We look forward to their being modified, corrected and more precisely determined as more experience is accumulated and shifted."

5. See sources cited in Note 1.

6. John P. Spiegel, "A Model for Relationships Among Systems," Roy R. Grinker, ed., *Toward a Unified Theory of Human Behavior* (New York: Basic Books, Inc., 1956), pp. 16-26.

7. Grinker, *op. cit.*

8. Melanie Klein, "On Identification," Klein, Paula Heiman, and Roger Money-Kyrle, eds., *New Directions in Psychoanalysis* (New York: Basic Books, Inc., 1954), Chap. 13. Elliott Jaques (see Klein, *et al.,* Chap. 20) agrees with Melanie Klein that Freud was aware of the process of identification by projection, although he was mainly interested in the process of identification by introjection. They quote his statement on love: "We see that the object is treated in the same way as our own ego, so that when we are in love a considerable amount of narcissistic libido overflows on the object. We love it on account of the perfections which we have striven to reach in our own ego." Melanie Klein comments further that "the process that Freud describes implies that this loved object is felt to contain the split-off loved, and valued part of the self which in this way continues its existence inside the object. It thereby becomes an extension of the self."

9. Klein, *op. cit.*

10. Anna Freud, *The Ego and the Mechanisms of Defense* (New York: International Universities Press, Inc., 1946), Chap. X.

11. Gerhart Piers and Milton B. Singer, *Shame and Guilt* (Springfield, Ill.: Charles C. Thomas, Publisher, 1953), differentiates between shame and guilt. Piers indicates that shame arises as a result of tension between the ego and the ego ideal rather than between the ego and superego, as in guilt. He further points out that guilt arises when transgression of the limits set by the superego actually occur or are contemplated. On the other hand, shame develops only when the ego does not live up to the expectations set by the ego ideal. Finally the unconscious fear in shame anxiety is that of being abandoned, whereas in guilt the fear is of mutilation. Piers delineates the ego ideal as containing a core of narcissistic omnipotence—a "too much" resulting in psychopathology in which the overinflated ideals often put the ego under unbearable stress. It also contains identifications with introjects of loving, reassuring aspects of the parent who gives permission to be like him. The clinically significant, narcissistically overexpectant parent leaves his image in these introjects. Furthermore, layers of later identifications with siblings, peers, social groups, or collective ideals further influence the structure of the ego ideal. Finally, Piers stresses the goals of the inherent "maturation drive," which results from the dynamic transaction between conscious and unconscious awareness of the ego's potentialities.

12. They have found useful a conceptual frame of reference using modified psychoanalytic concepts, notably the Sullivanian and Kleinian interpersonal transactional hypotheses in the diagnosis, therapy, and training of case workers for marital therapy. "The approach is by insight therapy which does not aim at 'guidance' such as giving advice or at manipulating the environment." See "Mental Hygiene of Marital Interaction," *Proceedings International Congress on Mental Health* (Paris, 1961), Group XVI, pp. 216-9; and Henry V. Dicks, "Object Relations Theory and Marital Studies," *British Journal of Medical Psychology*, 36 (1963), 125-9.

13. Alexander, "Psychoanalysis and Psychotherapy," Jules H. Masserman, ed., *Science and Psychoanalysis*, III. *Psychoanalysis and Human Values* (New York: Grune & Stratton, Inc., 1960), 250-9.

14. French, *The Integration of Behavior*, I, II (Chicago: University of Chicago Press, 1952-1953).

15. Greene and Solomon, "The Triangular Transference Transactions."

16. Alexander, "The Dynamics of Psychotherapy in Light of the Learning Theory," *American Journal of Psychiatry*, 120 (November, 1963), 440-8.

17. Greene and Solomon, "The Triangular Transference Transactions."

7

CONJOINT MARITAL THERAPY

Virginia M. Satir

For many years, the literature of social workers has been replete with references to joint interviewing of couples with marital problems. It was not until 1959, however, that Don D. Jackson first introduced the term "conjoint therapy" in psychiatric circles. In an excellent presentation in 1962, Andrew S. Watson succinctly described this approach at the annual meeting of the American Orthopsychiatric Association. Miss Satir was one of the discussants of that paper. She is endowed with ability both to comprehend quickly what is going on in the conjoint sessions and to think freely about the material in precise psychodynamic terms. The operational approach she advances in this chapter, which grows out of the work of a group at Palo Alto originally directed by Gregory Bateson, is based on the postulate, among others, that interpersonal relationships involve two levels of communication. The first is the message itself; the second involves one or more qualifying communications signaling how the message is to be interpreted. Communications at the first level are direct and explicit; those at the second are subtle and implicit. They are conveyed by the total context and by such nonverbal signals as voice tone and pace, facial expression, and the like. Miss Satir has further developed her concepts in her new book Conjoint Family Therapy.[1]

The concepts that underlie my treatment approach to marital therapy add up to a phenomenological theory of interpersonal behavior in which reality is validated by literal interactional negotiation. This theory means that any behavior that occurs between any two people is the product of both of them. The focus is on how to be personally authentic and spontaneous, which means how to encourage each person to commit himself to risk complete and uninhibited reporting of all that he feels and thinks, sees and hears about himself and any other person. I aim to demonstrate that everything can be understood once the premises from which any behavior is derived are made explicit and clear. I teach a method by which meaning can be given, received, and checked out without destroying oneself or another.

I believe that action is a separate negotiation, which follows after understanding is achieved. It is not an automatic follow-up of understanding. The manifestation of any thought or feeling therefore conveys nothing definitive about what will be done about it. That is another negotiation. For example, A's report in B's presence that he is angry says nothing definite about what he will do as a follow-up. It also says nothing definite about what B will do about A's report.

I expect to make three kinds of changes in each member of the marital pair: a change in his perception of himself and of others, which has both cognitive and affective parts; a change in his way of manifesting thoughts and feelings; and a change in his way of reacting to the stimulus and feedback of others. Briefly, these three parts form the patterns of interaction that compose the couple's "system." The couple's behavior both creates the system initially and, as experience accumulates, becomes the product of the system. Each system then becomes predictable through repetition. A set of behavioral rules inevitably develops, which may or may not be apparent to the members of the system. In any event, these rules become powerful shapers of each individual's behavior. I think that symptoms develop when the rules for operating do not fit needs for survival, growth, getting close to others, and productivity on the part of each member of the system.

My therapeutic efforts are designed to change the rules, which means changing the system. This aim requires that I be active and have an explicit and clear structure that will bring about change. I shall try to describe the structure, the premises underlying it, and the ways in which I use it.

Conjoint marital therapy is, by my definition, a therapeutic method in which both marital partners are seen together by the same therapist or by cotherapists, one male and one female, and in which the signaling symptom or condition is viewed by the therapist as a comment on the dysfunction of their interactional system.

I am talking about a marital pair *that has no children* and a pair that fits one or both of the following descriptions:

> One member has a psychiatric diagnosis of schizophrenia, delinquency, neurosis, or psychosomatic disorder.
> One or both members have a social diagnosis of alcoholism, gambling, extra-marital affairs, or inability to provide financially.

If the couple has children and the above conditions exist, I use the family therapeutic approach. I do so because, as a therapist, I believe I have an educational and preventive function, as well as a treatment function, for all the members of the family in which there is an identified patient or condition.

Returning to the marital pair, my treatment *process* is the same, regardless of whether the diagnosis is a psychiatric or a social one, because I believe the two are merely different ways of labeling dysfunctional processes. The dysfunctional condition is the result of dysfunctional communication processes, and it is the evidence of pain experienced by both members of the marital pair in their unsuccessful efforts to achieve joint outcomes.

In analyzing any outcome—a symptom is one kind of outcome—I use three major tools: a communication analysis, a model analysis, and a label or role-function analysis.

The therapist takes his diagnostic cues from his or her observation of the ways the couple has of communicating with each other. That is, he observes the ways in which the partners give and receive meaning and the ways in which each checks out meaning with the other. I call this observation *communication analysis*.

Briefly, *communication analysis* is made up of four parts. The first part involves who speaks, who speaks for whom, and who attributes blame or credit for his actions to someone else. The second part involves the "how" of getting messages across, which I call *congruency*. This congruency encompasses the matching of meaning in terms of the verbal symbols (language), voice tone and pace, facial expression, body position, and tonus. The third part involves what I call *delineation*. The term refers to how obvious, clear, and specific the verbal symbol is, the voice tone and pace, the facial expression, or the body position and tonus: How easily and clearly is the person heard and seen? The fourth part has to do with the *sequence* of four interchanges, that is, A's manifestation, B's response, A's response to B's response, and B's response to A's response to B.

By using these four aspects of communication analysis, I can see the method by which A and B attempt to give, receive, and check out meaning with each other. To the degree that meaning is not given or received clearly, specifically, and directly, validation of self and other (in terms of predictability, trust, and lovability) is potentially in question. One of the therapist's goals, then, is to make it possible for the couple to give, receive, and check out meaning, clearly, specifically, and directly. To go from being unclear, unspecific, and indirect to being clear, specific, and direct requires changes in one's ways of extending and maintaining self-esteem, one's use of feedback, and one's use of words.

From his observations of communication between the husband and wife, the therapist can make analytic and diagnostic inferences about the self-esteem and self-image of each. He can also observe the ways in which each person uses the other to increase his own low self-esteem and to complete his own self-image. From these inferences, further inferences can be drawn about individual processes for maintaining survival, continuing growth, and managing closeness to others.

I believe that all human beings are geared toward survival, growth, and getting close to others. Behavior that appears otherwise I believe is the result of what the person has concluded about his *chances* for survival, growth, and getting close to others. He has derived these conclusions over time from his perception of past experience. People who cannot openly manifest their wishes and abilities to survive, grow, and get close to others usually have a combined sense of littleness, powerlessness, incompetence, and absence of sexual delineation. All such people have difficulties with authority, autonomy, and sexuality, which are clearly revealed in their ways of communicating.

In an adult, feelings of low self-esteem are at variance with the common expectation that an adult will be big, powerful, competent, and sexually delineated (self-image). Each person is faced with closing the gap between his low self-esteem and how he would like to see himself. People in a dysfunctional situation usually have a wide gap. The dysfunctional person tries to close this gap through the other person, using overt or covert demands managed through guilt, anger, or helplessness.

In a dysfunctional pair, the husband uses the wife, and the wife uses the husband. The result is that neither receives gratification, and each feels himself being slowly strangled. Ensuing efforts to survive lead to symptomatic behavior and bring the couple to the therapist's office.

The goal of therapy is first to make explicit the means by which each uses the other to increase his own self-esteem, which I label the *parasitic operation,* and then to enable each to change those means so that he takes charge of maintaining it himself, rather than expecting it of his spouse. The goal is not to maintain the relationship nor to separate the pair but to help each to take charge of himself. Then people can manage their own outcomes: They decide for themselves whether to stay together or to separate.

Dr. Warren Brodey and others, including ourselves,* have found that mates in dysfunctional marital pairs see their spouses as they expect them to be, rather than as they are, and treat them accordingly. Because they cannot comment directly on the resulting situations, they rarely discover these expectations. The inevitable consequence is that each partner continually finds disappointment, which he experiences as betrayal or rejection. This process is manifest in accusation, attack, withdrawal, or acting out outside the

---

*The staff at the Mental Research Institute.

marriage. The marriage becomes a war, with a victor and a vanquished, a victim and a victimizer. The question is continually raised, overtly or covertly, of who is right, loved, sick, bad, stupid, or crazy. This continual questioning becomes self-perpetuating and acts as a predictable assault on both individuals' wavering self-esteem. When self-esteem is under assault, each individual's survival mechanisms are naturally activated.

Mate selection has long been recognized as fairly closely related to the male and female images that each spouse has developed in his growing-up years in his experience with his parents. That is, the basis for selecting a marital partner is linked to perceptions of the satisfactory or unsatisfactory outcomes of the interaction between parents, as well as perceptions of mother and father as separate and different entities. The image underlying the husband's expectation of how his wife should treat him and how he should treat his wife (and the wife's expectations of how her husband should treat her and how she should treat her husband) is derived initially from the interaction of his own parents as marital partners. It is also derived from the image of each parent in his role as parent to the child. I call the analysis of these images *model integration analysis*.

Model integration analysis involves the ways in which each child made room for the differentness of his parents and how he selected from them, as models, those things that would be useful and appropriate in his own development. As no human being is born with a set of instructions how to grow and develop, each child must take his cues and clues from those who are labeled his "teachers" for growing up, that is, his parents.

A child cannot discard recommendations from the adults around him as unfitting unless he is openly encouraged to experiment for "fit," with no penalty attached. Most adults do not realize that they serve as continuous models for their children. How they talk and act toward a child and toward others in his presence becomes material for the child's blueprint for his own behavior. Many adults are naive enough to think that a child takes from an adult only what the adult consciously directs toward the child. It is often a shattering experience for an adult to be confronted with a child's performance that matches what he considers an intolerable part of his own behavior.

We have found an amazing parallel between the interactions of the spouses in the families of origin and the interaction between the present marital pair. This parallel has led me to the conclusion that, in dysfunctional marital pairs, there is a continuing effort by marital partners to accomplish, through their relationship with each other, what was not accomplished in their families of origin.

This hypothesis may account for another observation: that the marital pair, although labeled husband and wife, are functioning in some form of parent-child or sibling-sibling relationship. For example, the husband-wife relationship resembles that between father and daughter, mother and son, or brother and sister. In the marriage, label and function are thus discrepant. I call this discrepancy the *role-function discrepancy*. It should not be hard to see that this situation leads to the presence of incongruence. There is an expectation of behavior that accommodates the perception of the label, and because of the way of operating there will also be behavior that fits the way the role is lived. These types of behavior do not match, and only confused behavioral messages can result.

In all dysfunctional marital pairs, neither partner has achieved the kind of change in his relationship with his own parents that would enable him to live as a colleague in the world of adults. As a result, dysfunctional marital pairs frequently live and function as children, with one or both sets of parents still in charge of their lives.

Through the use of the tools or instruments I have referred to as *communication analysis, model integration analysis,* and *role-function discrepancy analysis,* I am in a position to find clues that lead me in turn to an assessment of each individual's self-esteem and self-image. I work for the development of high self-esteem and a complete self-image, which show themselves in clear, specific, and direct communication between the partners.

I have isolated five processes that seem to me to furnish a universal and comprehensive base from which to design treatment plans:

Manifesting Self

"Manifesting self" means the ways in which one comments in the presence of another person about what he feels and thinks, sees and hears about himself and others. These ways may be described in three dimensions: congruence, delineation, and completeness. Congruence is the relationship among different ways of manifesting feeling: language, voice tone and pace, facial expression, body position, and tonus. "Delineation" refers to how obviously and clearly one speaks, looks, and acts. Completeness refers to the wholeness and specificity of the message.

The observer or the receiver of the manifestations of any person (the sender) evolve meaning from these three dimensions. The more congruent, obvious, and specific the manifestation is, the more it is possible for the receiver to grasp the explicit meaning intended by the sender. In my therapy with couples, I "check out" the receiver's conclusion about the intention of the sender, which makes it possible for me to help each toward clarity in giving and receiving meanings and in "checking them out" in their turn.

So often partners seem so sure of each other's reactions that they do not hear or see reactions that do not fit their expectations. Little change can come about such a situation until each is able to see and hear the other. A gross rule of thumb for separating functional from dysfunctional couples is to find their respective ways of matching current experience and previous expectation. The dysfunctional way is to tailor the current experience to fit the previous expectation, which obviously allows for no growth. The functional way is to reshape the expectation to fit current experience. A person with low self-esteem almost automatically acts dysfunctionally—I suspect because of anxiety engendered by venturing into something new. Although painful, the old is nevertheless familiar.

Separating Self from Other

This phrase refers to the ways in which each person recognizes the presence of the other's "skin boundaries" and the degree to which he acts on recognition that the other has a separate operating mechanism that runs on its own time. Indeed, it is sheer accident when the timing of one coincides with another in all situations.

My observation of the dysfunctional marital pair is that each member behaves as though the other should at all times match his own timing. Each behaves as if he expects the other to be hungry, to be thirsty, or to desire sex, recreation, or sleep at the identical times that he does himself. That their wishes are not identical raises questions of worth and lovability. Such questions seem related to perceptions that the condition of loving presupposes exact similarity of the loved one to the lover. Differentness, which is inevitable because of the uniqueness of every individual, is viewed as an assault on one's own lovability and worth. To fulfill an expectation of similarity then, uniqueness must be obliterated—but to obliterate the uniqueness of any individual is to risk his psychological death.

I take every opportunity to translate the concept of differentness, which is often used as a prelude to war, into a concept of uniqueness, which can be used as a stimulus to growth. This process essentially shows the gaps in the partners' perceptions of subject-object relationship.

Making Room for Self and Other

This process involves decision-making and is related to a universal human dilemma. A marital pair commits itself to the execution of joint outcomes like going to the movies together or having intercourse. Although the partners may agree on such an outcome, the question inevitably arises, Which movie and when? The dilemma is how can two people achieve a single outcome and still make room for the uniqueness of each? If each wants to see a different movie, who decides what both will do? What is the process of negotiation that makes it possible for them to be together in the same movie on the same evening?

There are several possibilities. One person can be decision-maker and the other capitulator. That is, the wife can go along with the husband (domineering husband and passive wife), or the husband can go along with the wife (domineering wife and passive, ineffectual husband). In these two cases, the uniqueness of one person may be by-passed. Alternatively, the two can fight openly until one wins by brute force (literal assault or, in its milder form, competition). In all these ways, the two can arrive at the same movie—but only at some cost to their self-esteem, their individual uniqueness, or their physical health. Another way to cope with this situation is to agree to go to separate movies. This solution may result in individual gratification, but it will be achieved at the expense of the hoped-for joint outcome—companionship—which was the original goal *vis-à-vis* isolation and distance. They can, of course, give up the idea of going to the movies at all and can stay home. Then a different joint outcome is achieved but perhaps at the expense of mutual joy, learning, or productivity.

Decision-making requires a tailoring process in which the shaving of one individual's autonomy does not result in feelings of attack on his self-esteem, in bodily injury, in feelings of isolation, or in personal deprivation. Instead, the process should enhance self-esteem, prevent bodily injury, create closeness, produce a feeling that the other is giving to him, and demonstrate productivity. These results come if the shaving of autonomy takes place within a context of *what fits* rather than of *who is right or boss*. In dysfunctional pairs, decision-making is usually done in terms of authority (who is right) rather than in terms of reality (what fits).

Ways in Which Differentness Is Acknowledged

If each member of a marital pair can comment openly on what he feels, thinks, sees, and hears about himself and the other, if each can treat the other as a separate being in search of real matching of "life needs," and if joint outcomes can be achieved through negotiating for what fits, then the acknowledgment of and reaction to the presence of any differences is that of search and exploration. Functional and fitting outcomes are assured.

If members cannot comment openly, however, if each expects to be a duplicate of the other, and if each in turn arrives at joint outcomes through power tactics, then the acknowledgment of differences must be avoided. To acknowledge difference is to raise the question of worth. Joint outcomes will consequently be chaotic, unpredictable, inappropriate, ungratifying, and unrealistic.

The Ways Joint Outcomes Are Achieved

These ways offer opportunities to assess the processes connected with self-esteem and self-images. Inappropriate or incomplete outcomes can be used as clues to the ways in which each person tries to raise his self-esteem and to complete his self-image.

In this discussion, I have defined by implication my treatment goals. My therapeutic interventions are aimed at changing the processes of coping for each individual, which in turn alters the system for both individuals and is reflected in their new ways of communicating and in their increased productivity.

To make these changes possible, the therapist must make

fuller use of self than is usually the case. I divide the utility of the therapist into three major parts. The first is that of *a device* that reports fully what it sees and hears and how it interprets what it sees and hears. Often therapists report their interpretations, which are their conclusions from what they see and hear. They do not, however, provide the evidence from which these conclusions have been drawn. This omission contributes to the patient's vulnerability to harm, for what any one person sees and hears is, to a great degree, idiosyncratic. In my opinion, the failure of some therapists to report fully what they see and hear is responsible for much of what they describe as resistance by patients. To reduce further the patient's puzzlement about what the therapist means, the therapist should report clearly, directly, specifically, and as completely as possible.

In the process of reporting, the therapist acts as a *model of communication*. In this role, I can ask and tell, that is, I can demonstrate how to ask questions and to negotiate for meaning. In this process, I enable any other two to ask, tell, and check out.

This experience can serve as an ego-enhancing corrective and eventually reflects itself in clearer, more specific, and more direct communication between husband and wife. By commenting on anything and everything that seems obvious, I encourage patients to give up fears of dangerous information. Anything that comes up in the way of content can be viewed in terms of the processes of communication; integrating models; delineating roles; sorting out past, present, and future implications of present events; developing self-esteem and self-images; and achieving outcomes. And these elements are all in the interest of survival, growth, getting close to others, and being productive.

As a *resource person*, finally, I have special knowledge that, if my treatment is successful, my marital pair can share and use.

I enter the therapeutic situation with the expectation that change is possible and with a clear, delineated structure for encouraging change. This structure embraces concepts of communication, interpersonal and intrapersonal con-structs, self-esteem, and self-image. It is a structure in which the therapist actively intervenes, completely reports, asks for complete reports, acts as a model of communication, and gives freely of his or her own resources. By doing so, the therapist enables the marital pair to identify and use its own resources.

NOTES

1. Virginia M. Satir, *Conjoint Family Therapy* (Palo Alto: Science and Behavior Books, Inc., 1964).

8

TREATMENT OF
MARITAL DISHARMONY:

The Use of Individual, Concurrent, and
Conjoint Sessions as a "Combined Approach"

Bernard L. Greene, Betty P. Broadhurst,
and Noel Lustig

This paper presents another technical approach in the treatment of
marital discord as utilized by a psychoanalyst, a social worker, and
a psychiatrist. Miss Broadhurst is an outstanding therapist and
teacher of social work. Her techniques with the "combined ap-
proach" are presented in this chapter. Doctor Lustig describes the
"combined approach" as utilized by a psychiatrist. He has worked
closely with the senior author.

The "combined approach" in the treatment of marital disharmony utilizes individual, concurrent, and conjoint sessions in various purposeful combinations. Due to the marked
variability in marital patterns and the unpredictable therapeutic course, technical variations become desirable. In this
approach, both partners are treated by the same therapist.[1]
The treatment process is based on a plan of active support,
including environmental manipulation; complementary
goals; clarification of role expectations and enactments;
redirection of intrapsychic and interpersonal energies; and
evocation of "healthier" communication. The operational
approach is carried out within a framework of psychoanalytic constructs blended with small-group,[2] communicational,[3] and learning-theory concepts.[4]

An increasing number of therapists[5] is beginning to
devote more attention to multipersonal approaches to the
treatment of marital disharmony. The work of some group
therapists[6] has much to offer to the student of the "combined

approach." As more and more therapists of the several disciplines use multiperson interviews, we notice the gradual development of new therapeutic techniques shared by all of them. Should this process continue, the outcome may well be better interdisciplinary communication and understanding, in addition to a broader range of treatment possibilities and greater acceptance of multipersonal approaches. This possibility does not mean that psychoanalytically oriented one-to-one therapy is to be replaced, but it does promise greater latitude for therapists in the choice of treatment methods most suited to the problems of particular couples.

A triadic or conjoint approach to therapy differs in many ways from a dyadic approach. Some of these differences are basic and are related to the patient's and to the therapist's views of dyadic and triadic interviews. When dyadic *and* triadic sessions are combined, the form of the interview takes on additional and special meanings for the participants. Perhaps at this point we can identify more specifically the basis for some of the concepts that have been integrated into this approach.

General Concepts[7]

The form of the "combined approach" represents various aspects of functioning in the marital relationship. A "human being" may be regarded as incorporating three separate systems: an *individual system* composed of intrapsychic events, an *interpersonal system*[8] involving transactions "with significant others," and a *societal system* responding to an interplay of forces between the individual and society. The three systems are reflected in the "combined approach" through the use of dyadic and triadic sessions, which alternately focus on the individual spouse and the marriage. The process of treatment demonstrates the therapist's dual concern with understanding the origin of feelings in the past and their re-enactment in current marital transactions.

Communication. In triadic sessions, the aim is to eliminate incongruity, doubt, and distortions from *communication* so that implicit and explicit meanings and messages
become identical. This process provides couples with common communicational systems on which to base their treatment. The opportunity to experience multiple environments
in combined therapy points up the contrast between individual and multipersonal relationships and brings out
different sides of the personality that could well be lost in
individual treatment. It has been said that there is a tendency for therapists to make the mistake of assuming that a
person will behave in the same way in all situations.[9] The
opportunity for feedback through the use of dyadic and
triadic sessions furnishes a corrective for the therapist's
misperceptions and misinterpretations. One advantage of
combined therapy, then, is to increase the perceptive awareness of all participants.

Dyadic versus Triadic Treatment Situations. Within this
matrix, we can now take a closer look at the dyadic and
triadic sessions. The psychoanalytic concepts of determinism,
analysis of resistances, and the unconscious are basic premises. The dyadic sessions reflect the importance of the
intrapsychic structure of each partner. Psychoanalytic theory
is concerned primarily with internal conflicts of which the
patient is unaware. In the dyadic hour, what comes to the
fore is the patient's more deeply rooted personality com-
ponents, whereas, in the triadic setting, the "intersocial
reality" comes into focus. These two settings offer opportunities to work through different analytical material more
adequately, material that is complementary. The utilization
of multifocal transference phenomena continues to be a
cornerstone in the operational approach of the senior author.

The living experience of the triadic session is an important phenomenon. Experiencing the difference between
the dyadic and triadic situations, being treated differently,
being reacted to differently, and observing the repercussions
of one's behavior and verbalizations on two other individuals or its interpretations by the therapist stimulate a

desire to understand one's reactions.[10] The triadic interviews thus promote tolerance for the other person's uniqueness and integrity and represent a shift from "ego centered private fields to fields of mutual orientation."[11]

In the triadic interview, the transactions of the partners can be experienced in their healthy and unhealthy aspects. The significance of inappropriate behavior can be clarified on the spot. Failures of the individual partners in perception, interpretation of perceptions, communication, and interpersonal behavior become the material that is repeatedly worked through during the sessions. In the triangular setting, the therapist witnesses the unfolding of the conflicts *in situ,* which enables him to understand the dynamics much better. Feelings of anger may erupt, but the presence of the therapist helps to soften as well as to exploit them for understanding and tolerance.

The triangular setting activates the old family conflicts of each partner, who tends to act them out in the therapeutic situation. It is thus possible to see more clearly the unfolding *projection* of these conflictual situations onto both the therapist and the partner. Furthermore, one can observe the manner in which each partner provokes his mate to play desired or needed transference roles. Naturally, the couple re-experiences its original family conflicts but in a different atmosphere, one conducive to learning and "growing up." As the partners are able to turn more to each other for understanding and support, the therapist's position becomes superfluous. Once meaningful communication has been achieved, the partners are in command of the tools necessary to work out their problems and to make problem-solving a joint endeavor.

Each spouse must be moderately secure in his own identity if he is to accept appropriate roles; to complement and support the partner; to evolve a workable communicational system; and to operate flexibly, under changing conditions, to achieve common goals. The dyadic sessions provide opportunities to trace the development of the self-image from reflected appraisals by significant adults, principally parents, a concept expertly stated by Sullivan[12] and others. If the parents' appraisals are based on their own neurotic distortions and are derogatory rather than accepting, the child, lacking experience and judgment, will incorporate these appraisals and develop a negative self-image. In the triadic sessions, the impact of the negative self-image on the interpersonal relationship of the couple is pointed out. Interpretations to both that this factor is disturbing the marital relationship can be valuable in improving the marriage. Furthermore, as both mates begin to understand the ways in which they operate toward each other because of their poor self-images, pressure for change develops. The next step involves bringing into focus and utilization, as much as possible, the positive and creative aspects of the partners.

The Therapist in the Triadic Treatment Situation. The triangular setting is more demanding of the *therapist's* observational span, for he must recognize both partners' mental continuity in the framework of a transactional field. His personality exerts a strong impact on the couple. He must therefore be capable of warmth, "emphatic neutrality,"[13] and sensitivity. These factors are as important as his frame of reference. He can set an example for identification. His attitude should be one that encourages self-esteem, that develops and strengthens the ego, and helps to clarify the self-image. There should be no lecturing or preaching but open discussion. This atmosphere enables the couple to think through its own value systems and to develop more realistic values as effective guides for behavior.

There are so many things happening simultaneously in the triadic session that only by *selective* attention to some problems can the therapist avoid becoming confused. He finds trends for his own orientation and for his interpretations of the couple's mutual responses.

The triangular setting and the face-to-face confrontation of the partners necessitate greater activity on the part of the therapist and greater use of the freer aspects of his own personality. A more effective transactional field therefore ensues because there is less narcissistic reinforcement of illness. It is in this area that the triadic operational approach makes perhaps its greatest contribution.

Indications for Combined Therapy

1. Initial evaluation of the couple indicating
   a. a need for triadic sessions to manipulate the marital relationship in order to achieve greater harmony
   b. a need for dyadic sessions for entrenched personal conflicts.
2. Failure of the conjoint or concurrent techniques to alleviate hostility that has reached explosive proportions between the spouses.
3. Acting out by one or both spouses that cannot be dealt with by the concurrent or conjoint approaches.
4. A patient's obsessive-compulsive personality pattern that makes it necessary to enlist the co-operation of the partner.
5. A couple that can perceive relationships between events and its own responses *only* when actually confronted with them.[14]
6. A spouse's relationship with a single parent introjected to the degree that he is threatened by a dyadic setting (Individual therapy alone may activate conflicts, overwhelming the spouse with fear of his sexual, hostile, or oral dependent needs.)
7. A therapeutic impasse in concurrent therapy because of transference difficulties that may be of two types: either too intense or involving insufficient emotional involvement of the patient (The patient's aggressive and demanding sexual or dependent attitudes are subject in the conjoint sessions to dilution; the previously overemotional transference situation in the individual session becomes more manageable, and analytic therapy can then be continued more successfully. On the other hand, the emotionally detached patient, who likes to intellectualize as a main defense and can make himself quite comfortable in his individual sessions, will provoke his partner to express his irritation at this behavior.)
8. A therapeutic impasse occurs in dyadic sessions because the dyadic transference neurosis can be activated and interpreted only in the triadic sessions.[15]

Contraindications for Combined Therapy

1. One spouse who prefers to see a therapist without his partner.
2. One spouse who is markedly psychotic. (This contraindication is

questionable, and we believe that in some cases psychosis is an indication for combined therapy.)

3. A case involving privileged communications of which the partner is not aware—infidelity, homosexuality, and so forth.
4. Inability of one or both spouses, because of emotional immaturity, to share the same therapist.
5. One mate who has a twin who has caused severe competitive problems in the past and will complicate the therapy.

These contraindications (as well as the indications) for combined therapy are relative and are all subject to change with increasing clinical experience and knowledge.

Therapeutic Operational Approaches

An important advantage of the combined approach is its flexibility; it lends itself to both the styles of various therapists and the marked variability of marital patterns. We shall describe the techniques of three different disciplines: social casework, psychiatry, and psychoanalysis.

SOCIAL CASEWORK

The stage is set for treatment on an interactional basis at the time of the first phone call for an appointment. The expectation that both partners will come, at least for an initial evaluation, assures, almost without exception, that both will appear. The clearly stated focus on the marriage strongly influences the expectations and the approach of the therapist, as well as of the partners. The rationale is that no problem can exist that does not affect both partners and that solutions must come from both together. From the beginning, an individual partner is thus released from sole responsibility, and the stage is set for both partners to look at the interaction between them and to experience what help may come from therapy without committing themselves beyond the initial visit. The rationale continues with an ego-supportive focus—appreciating influences of the past, noting abilities today, but underlining responsibilities for tomorrow. This diversion of responsibility for marital conflict from the partners as individuals frees each (to different degrees) of some of the guilt he carries. The results are less need to accuse or defend and better ability to understand the spouse by helping to identify how current responses have their roots in behavior learned in the past.

The process of treatment is based on the idea of making the first interview a sample of the total process. It is termed a "conference," *which connotes an interactional process in which the contributions of each person are valued.* The partners are seen together, then individually, then together again. Usually two hours are allowed for the total evaluation conference, but the exact division of time is essentially "played by ear." As a guide, twenty minutes might be planned for the initial "joint" interview, during which the problems are presented by the couple together; this early opportunity to "feel" the marital interaction provides helpful cues for the individual sessions. The cues come from observing how the partners behave in the waiting room, who initiates the interview, and how the decision is made as to who will have the first individual session. A beginning picture of the communicational and interactional patterns, at least before a stranger and under stress, is obtained.

The individual sessions may last thirty or forty minutes apiece. The aim is to obtain a brief family history in order to identify possible precursors of "then and now" misunderstandings. Taking histories is viewed as part of the treatment process, and the focus is therefore less on facts and more on feelings about the parents, the parents' marriage, the siblings, and the alignments in the family. An attempt is made to get "egos engaged": What the therapist says is on an ego level aligned with that of the partner. A great interest is shown in what the partner says, although it is not played up or down. Concern and interest serve as an early cornerstone of alliance. The content, although diagnostically helpful, may actually be less important than the manner in which it is elicited and the way in which the therapist relates as the material is presented.

How each partner perceives his early years and life history begins to clarify his perception pattern, the "glasses" through which he views the world, the marriage, and his partner. The therapist also attempts an empathic relationship with each partner, which aims at providing a role model that will not duplicate early unhappy relationships but can be used to reassure the partners that the present need not repeat the past. To the extent that the therapist-patient relationship can be kept relatively unentangled from negative feelings, the therapist can also be used as an "other"[16] who makes explicit the feelings aroused by implicit behavior.

The final brief joint interview after the individual sessions illustrates that, although the therapist has an interest and concern in each partner separately, the overriding concern is their interaction in marriage. The sequence also typifies the over-all plan of combined individual and conjoint sessions. The opportunity to see both partners at the end permits a "shaping" of what has transpired in the individual conferences, a recapitulation of the importance of individual patterns as they merge in the marriage. The therapist's confidence that the partners can work on indicated changes is partly conveyed by his leaving as many decisions as possible about the timing of individual and conjoint sessions to them and by his confronting them immediately with such "interactional tasks" as who will pay and when and who will come what day and time.

The therapeutic process is based on single, concurrent, and joint interviews. That is, each week each partner has an individual session, which is essentially the same as concurrent therapy. Every third week there is a conjoint session, with both partners and the therapist. The combination can be flexible from the start, which means that the therapist can begin with concurrent therapy and plan the first conjoint session for a time when each partner feels prepared; he can schedule it monthly in addition to the individual sessions; or he can substitute it for the individual sessions every third week. Couples who must come some distance for interviews or who have financial difficulties often find that they prefer primarily conjoint interviews, with individual sessions when special needs arise. Conceptually we might view the specific combination of single and joint interviews as a point on a scale, with all "singles" at one end and all "joints" at the other. The single interview can be viewed as filling the individual's need for the therapist's total attention, a need reminiscent of the parent-child relationship. The joint interview can be visualized as a co-operative venture between partners able to tackle their problems together, to find support and reassurance from one another, and to share the therapist.

PSYCHIATRY

The opening maneuver is the same for both the psychiatrist and the psychoanalyst. The philosophy of therapy is spelled out in the initial phone call when we *insist* that the couple be interviewed together at least once during the diagnostic phase. We feel that separate interviews at the beginning are essential in order to elicit privileged communications. Our routine procedure is explained to each. It begins with an evaluative phase (to obtain psychopathological and psychosocial profiles) consisting of one to three individual interviews, a conjoint interview, and a biographical marital questionnaire to be filled out at home if possible. The last covers the history of the marriage from its beginning to the present. A routine battery of psychological tests is administered when indicated.

The evaluative-diagnostic phase is naturally followed by a treatment plan. The couple is specifically told that there are a number of techniques, which will be changed if necessary, depending upon the clinical course and the judgment of the therapist.

In the psychiatric sessions, all interviews are conducted in the upright face-to-face position. The technique is that of psychoanalytically oriented psychotherapy. The focus is on the current marital situation as influenced by the past events, needs, and feelings of each spouse. The level of anxiety or hostility and hope is maintained at a point of maximum ego integration by interpretations, environmental manipulation, reassurance, persuasion, and so forth. If necessary, tranquilizers or antidepressants are used. When indicated, daily diaries are used as sources of data on the conscious intent and feelings of the couple, which are useful in determining the nature of motivations and responses.

Whereas in the dyadic sessions the focus is on both intrapsychic and interpersonal phenomena, in the triadic sessions interpretations focus principally on those aspects of material and dynamics that relate to the communication process between the spouses. One of the principal tactical advantages of the triadic session "lies in the fact that it is possible to make an interpretation to one spouse, though its main impact is directed toward the other one. If there is strong resistance or ego vulnerability in one, a correlate interpretation can be to the other spouse, thus turning the interlooking nature of the marital neurosis to therapeutic advantage."[17]

Each dyadic session lasts fifty minutes, and the frequency varies from one to three interviews a week. The triadic sessions last from one to one and one-half hours. Because of the large amount of material reported, it is difficult to confine this type of session to fifty minutes. The interpretive focus should be shifted back and forth between the partners, so that the sessions end with each receiving approximately equal attention from the therapist. When time is available, two fifty-minute sessions are scheduled. We prefer to see each couple once a week in a triadic meeting, but at times we can see them only twice a month. There is great flexibility, however, and the couple is given permission to telephone at any time. Not infrequently, emergency evening and Sunday sessions are necessary. The seating arrangements and attitudes of the partners are an important observational point. Do they vie for the closest position to the therapist, do they sit together and work as a unit, and so forth?

An important task for the psychiatrist in the triadic sessions is the interpretation of the "ego states" (parent, adult, child) of the individuals. Hopefully, the "adult ego state" can be helped, through clarifications, to dominate the marital interaction of both patients. Often, seeing the archaic responses in their mates lets people explore their own responses. Also, one partner's "child" response patterns often force the other partner into inappropriate responses to maintain the marriage. These clarifications of unconscious *wishes,* which may be different from verbalized wishes, are *very important* in the treatment process.[18]

PSYCHOANALYSIS

The psychoanalyst has an additional tool when intensive depth therapy is indicated—the psychoanalytic situation. The triadic sessions are fairly standardized, but great flexibility is possible in the dyadic sessions. One partner may receive supportive psychotherapy while the other is analyzed; both may be analyzed synchronously; both may receive psychotherapy; one may receive psychotherapy, while the other participates only in the triadic sessions; or one may be in analysis, while the other participates only in the triadic sessions.

In the triadic sessions, the partners sit upright facing the therapist, who usually sits equidistant between them at the apex of a triangle, which makes for easier observation of the couple. In the dyadic sessions, either the upright or the couch position is used, depending on the clinical material. For example, with a woman who has an aggressive personality with frigidity, the couch position is usually insisted upon.

In the psychoanalytic approach, dream material is utilized extensively in both the dyadic and triadic sessions, affording valuable insights not only into each partner's personality organization and behavior patterns but also into the marital transactions. Dreams reported in the triadic sessions provide verification and clarity of understanding of the marital transactions and also of the various levels of transference phenomena, both dyadic and triadic. In the triadic interviews, we observe how the ideas of one spouse elicit reactions in the partner. Although one partner may continue to discuss his mate's ideas, soon his own unconscious feelings and thoughts gain the upper hand and reveal his true attitudes and bring to light areas of conflict. This type of communication makes possible a new dimension in understanding the couple. At the end of the session, we usually summarize or add a more comprehensive interpretation.

We have been influenced in our approach to dreams by Thomas M. French's[19] neo-Freudian view that dreams have an important problem-solving function. We seek in both the manifest and latent content of the dreams information on attempts by the ego to solve the marital conflicts. The couples are invariably intrigued by their dreams. When there is a lull in the session, which is extremely rare in the triadic setting, dreams offer points of departure for communication, an advantage of this type of therapy. A dream may be as important in the dyadic session as in the triadic. Managing the therapeutic situation poses many problems. Of major consideration is how far the analyst should take one partner through the intricacies of the other's analysis. Some aspects of this problem are the technique of handling psychological interpretations, which interpretations already given to one spouse should be repeated to the other, what interpretations should be withheld, and so forth. The frequency of sessions is determined by both the flow of clinical material and the emotional level of the marital relationship.

Summary

Combined therapy is a useful therapeutic tool when both triadic and dyadic transactions are necessary, in the opinion of the therapist, either for successful treatment of the marital transaction or of one of the partners. This usefulness is recognized by therapists in three disciplines, *social work, psychiatry,* and *psychoanalysis.* The form and character of the treatment processes using these different treatment settings are to some extent determined by the training and goals of the different disciplines.

In essence, conjoint sessions serve several purposes. Diagnostically, they enable the therapist to identify the point of disharmony, its basis, and each partner's part in its creation and resolution. Intermittently they enable a gauging of the couple's progressive abilities to relate and communicate. They provide a reality check on any fantasy relationships envisioned by either partner with the therapist. They provide a check for the therapist on any misconceptions arising from the individual interviews. Seeing the partners together often reveals unexpected strengths or resources that might otherwise remain unrecognized. Behavior patterns that are quite obvious in the individual sessions may be quite different in the joint situation. The goal of achieving compatibility or equilibrium is more obvious when both partners are present.

One of the strongest factors in favor of combined therapy is the meaning to both partners and to the therapist of focusing on an institution larger than either individual partner. Implicitly and explicitly this focus highlights the mutual responsibility of the partners for their communication and transactional patterns. The advantage of the combined approach is the opportunity to gauge individuals' needs for total attention and to provide it, while always keeping in sight the reality of the marriage, which encourages growing up. The model gives recognition to individual personalities but focuses on aspects that would complement one another harmoniously and find equilibrium if merged. A final advantage is the flexibility of the model, which lends itself to the styles of various therapists and to the personalities and situations of various married couples.

NOTES

1. For the purposes of this chapter, there is no need to differentiate the special areas of competence of the various disciplines. For simplicity, practitioners of no matter which discipline will be referred to

as "therapist," and the type of activity carried out will be identified as "therapy" (whether it be psychotherapy, marital counseling, multi-client interviewing, psychoanalysis, or any other). The latter term does not imply any particular level of treatment. It does imply a "type" of treatment and is used to differentiate individual from multiperson treatment when the focus is on marriage. Furthermore, in this chapter, one-to-one sessions will be referred to as *dyadic* and conjoint sessions as *triadic*.

2. Alfred R. Lindesmith and Anselm Strauss, *Social Psychology* (Rev. ed.; New York: Dryden Press, 1956); Fritz Heider, *Psychology of Interpersonal Relations* (New York: John Wiley & Sons, Inc., 1958); Solomon E. Asch, *Social Psychology* (Englewood Cliffs, N.J.: Prentice-Hall, Inc., 1952); and J. D. Matarazzo, "Prescribed Behavior Therapy: Suggestions from Interview Research," A. R. Barnasch, ed., *Experimental Foundations of Clinical Psychology* (New York: Basic Books, Inc., 1962).

3. Jurgen Ruesch, *Therapeutic Communication* (New York: W. W. Norton & Company, Inc., 1963).

4. Orval H. Mowrer, *Learning Theory and Personality Dynamics* (New York: The Ronald Press Company, 1950); and Franz Alexander, "The Dynamics of Psychotherapy in Light of Learning Theory," *American Journal of Psychiatry*, 120 (1963), 440-8.

5. See Nathan W. Ackerman, Frances L. Beatman, and Sanford H. Sherman, eds., *Exploring the Base for Family Therapy* (New York: Family Service Association of America, 1961); M. Robert Gomberg, "Family Oriented Treatment of Marital Problems," Cora Kasius, ed., *Social Casework in the Fifties* (New York: Family Service Association of America, 1962), pp. 198-212; Ernest N. Gullerud and Virginia Lee Harlan, "Four-Way Joint Interviewing in Marital Counseling," *Social Casework*, 43 (December, 1962), 532-7; Eugenia Huneus, "A Dynamic Approach to Marital Problems," *Social Casework*, 44 (March, 1963), 142-8; Miriam Jolesch, "Casework Treatment of Young Married Couples," *Social Casework*, 43 (May, 1962), 245-51, Gisela Konopka, "Group Work Techniques in Joint Interviewing," National Conference of Social Workers *Social Welfare Forum* (New York: Columbia University Press, 1957); Dwaine R. Lindberg and Anne W. Wosmek, "The Use of Family Sessions in Foster Home Care," *Social Casework*, 44 (March, 1963), 137-41; Otto Pollak and Donald Brieland, "The Midwest Seminar on Family Diagnosis and Treatment," *Social Casework*, 42 (July, 1961), 319-24; Frances H. Scherz, "Multiple-Client Interviewing: Treatment Implications," *Social Casework*, 43 (March, 1962), 120-5; Pauline M. Shereshefsky, "Family Unit Treatment in Child Guidance," *Social Work*, 8 (October, 1963), 4; Helen S. Sholtis, "Management of Marriage Counseling Cases," *Social Casework*, 45 (February, 1964), 71-8; Rex A. Skidmore, "The Joint Interview in

Marriage Counseling," *Marriage and Family Living*, 17 (1955), 4;
Alexander Thomas, "Simultaneous Psychotherapy with Marital Part-
ners," *American Journal of Psychotherapy*, 10 (October, 1956), 716-27;
Sue Vesper, "Casework Aimed at Supporting Marital Role Reversal,"
Social Casework, 43 (June, 1962), 303-7; Viola W. Weiss, "Multiple-
Client Interviewing: An Aid in Diagnosis," *Social Casework*, 43
(March, 1962), 14; and Carl A. Whitaker, "Psychotherapy with
Couples," *American Journal of Psychotherapy*, 12 (January, 1958),
18-23.

6. See E. Fried, "Combined Group and Individual Therapy with
Passive-Narcissistic Patients," *International Journal of Group Psycho-
therapy*, 5 (1955), 194-203; Oscar Guttman, "The Dynamic Shift of
Transference in Combined Individual and Group Analysis," *Journal
of Psychoanalysis in Groups*, 1 (1962), 76-82; James Jackson and
Martin Grotjahn, "The Treatment of Oral Defenses by Combined
Individual and Group Psychotherapy," *International Journal of Group
Psychotherapy*, 8 (1958), 373-82; Asya L. Kadis and Max Markowitz,
"Group Psychotherapy," *Progress in Clinical Psychology*, 3 (New York:
Grune & Stratton, Inc., 1958), pp. 154-83; D. M. Lipshutz, "Combined
Group and Individual Psychotherapy," *American Journal of Psycho-
therapy*, 11 (1957), 336-44; Helen Papenek, "Combined Group and
Individual Therapy in Private Practice," *American Journal of Psycho-
therapy*, 8 (1954), 679-86; Clifford J. Sager, "Concurrent Individual
and Group Analytic Psychotherapy," *American Journal of Orthopsy-
chiatry*, 30 (1960), 225-41; Sager, "The Effects of Group Therapy on
Individual Psychoanalysis," *International Journal of Group Psychotherapy*, 9 (1959), 403-19; and Emanuel K. Schwartz and Alexander
Wolf, "Psychoanalysis in Groups: Some Comparisons with Individual
Analysis," *Journal of General Psychology*, 64 (1961), 153-91.

7. Asch, *op. cit.*; Fritz Reider, "Perceiving the Other Person," Ren-
ato Taguiri and Luigi Petrullo, eds., *Person Perception and Interpersonal Behavior* (Stanford: Stanford University Press, 1958), p. 30;
and George H. Mead, *Mind, Self and Society* (Chicago: University of
Chicago Press, 1934), p. 47, have been particularly helpful in formu-
lating some of the material in this section.

8. James L. Tichener, Thomas D'Zmura, Myra Golden, and Richard
Emerson, "Family Transaction and Derivation of Individuality," *Family Process*, 2 (March, 1963), 95-120.

9. Heider, *op. cit.*, p. 1.

10. R. Lippitt and A. Hubbe, "Role Playing for Personnel and
Guidance Workers: Review of Literature with Suggestions for Application," *Group Psychotherapy*, 9 (1956), 89-114.

11. Asch, *op. cit.*, p. 163.

12. Harry Stack Sullivan, *The Interpersonal Theory of Psychiatry*
(New York: W. W. Norton & Company, Inc., 1953).

13. Scherz, *op. cit.*

14. Arthur A. Miller and Melvin Sabshin, "Psychotherapy in Psychiatric Hospitals," *Archives of General Psychiatry,* 9 (1963), 56.

15. Jackson and Grotjahn, *op. cit.*

16. Mead, *op. cit.,* p. 47.

17. Andrew S. Watson, "The Conjoint Psychotherapy of Marriage Partners," *American Journal of Orthopsychiatry,* 33 (November, 1963), 912-21.

18. We have found Eric Berne's concepts of structural and transactional analysis to be most helpful therapeutically. Patients, in our experience, readily grasp and, most important, are able to apply in their marriages the awareness not only of their current ego states but also of those of their spouses, especially as seen in the "game of uproar." See Eric Berne, *Transactional Analysis in Psychotherapy: A Systematic Individual and Social Psychiatry* (New York: Grove Press, 1961).

19. Thomas M. French, *The Integration of Behavior, I. Basic Postulates* (Chicago: University of Chicago Press, 1952).

9

THE FAMILY APPROACH TO MARITAL DISORDERS

Nathan W. Ackerman

Doctor Ackerman is one of the outstanding pioneers in the family-centered approach to mental illness, having anticipated the current significant trend in family diagnosis and therapy many years ago. His interest in this area stems from study of unsolved problems in the psychiatry of children and adults, in psychoanalytic theory and practice, in individual and group psychotherapy, in the relations between personality and psychosomatic illness, and in the psychology of prejudice. In some of these fields, he has worked closely with social scientists. He was a founder of the first family mental health clinic in this country, is now director of the professional program of the Family Institute, and is chairman of the Board of Editors of Family Process. *He has published extensively on the theory and practice of family psychotherapy. Doctor Ackerman believes "that an accurate understanding of the unconscious and of transference is possible only as these dynamics are matched not only to the realities of the analyst's person but also to the conscious organization of the person's experience, the total integrative patterns of personality and the prevailing realities of contemporary life." His book,* The Psychodynamics of Family Life, *is must reading for anyone who would treat marital problems.*

It is common knowledge today that the social institution of marriage is not working as we should like it to. To be sure, the institution of marriage is here to stay, but it is not the same any more. It is rickety; its joints creak. It threatens to crack wide open. Although marriage may be ordained in heaven, it is surely falling apart on earth, at least in our part of the world. Three generations survey the record with dismay. The older married folks look down with silent reproach on the younger ones. The younger married folks look at themselves in shock and perplexity and wonder how on earth they got this way. The children look at their parents, not with reverent respect, but with bitter accusation. They indict their parents: "You are wrecking our family. What are you doing to yourselves and to us? You are failing miserably. Why?"

In the present-day community, anxiety about the instability of marriage and family is widespread. The sources of worry are the "side-wise" marriage, the teen-age marriage, infidelity, desertion, divorce, multiple marriages, the loosening of sex standards, the war between the sexes, "momism," the weakness of fathers, the reduction of parental authority, the broken home, emotionally injured children, the anarchy of youth, and the trend toward delinquency. With all these problems comes a growing disillusionment with the tradition and sentiment of marriage and family.

If today the marriage bond is unstable, it is because the entire constellation of the contemporary family is itself unstable. As our way of life at all levels—family, community, and culture—is in a state of flux, the style of marriage must also echo the profound currents of change and instability.

Healing forces do emerge, but the healing itself is often warped. It is analogous to what surgeons call "the pathological healing" of a wound. For a multiplicity of reasons, we are challenged to take a new look at this old problem and, if possible, to discover a fresh approach to the marital disorders of our time.

For me, a psychiatric clinician, the marital problem poses a tantalizing challenge, comparable to that of a complicated jigsaw puzzle. We find one part that fits; instantly we hope and expect that all the others will fall quickly into place and reveal the hidden design; but it is not so easy.

Marriage is more than sex; it is a whole way of life. It is a joining together in the work, joys, and sadnesses of life. Disorders of the marital relationship cannot be understood in a social vacuum. The fit or lack of fit of the partners can be properly appraised only within the framework of the family viewed as an integrated behavior system with dominant values and a definable organizational pattern. The marital adaptation must be seen within that larger network of relationships that reflects the identity connections of each partner with his family of origin and with the larger community. Relevant beyond sexual union are the basic functions of family that have to do with security, child-rearing, social training, and the development of the marriage partners both as a couple and as individuals.

To illustrate: A social worker of twenty-four years, married six months, was considering divorce. In the initial psychiatric interview, try as I might, I could not find the slightest hint of her motive. Why divorce? Finally, in desperation, I asked, "Is it your sex life? What in the world is wrong?"

"Oh, no," she said, "my husband is an expert lover. Believe me, sexual intercourse is just great. The only trouble is that there is no verbal intercourse at all." Diagnosis: physical relations, good; emotional interchange, none. The complaint of "silent treatment" in married life is a frequent one these days.

Interviewing another couple, a kewpie doll of a wife and a big, burly police captain of a husband, I had a different experience. This couple had been married ten years and had three children. The wife threatened divorce. She was cute, childlike, but she breathed fire. She let loose a barrage of bitter accusations. For the better part of an hour her husband sat mute; he could not get a word in edgewise. What was her complaint? Her husband had cheated her out of her rights as a woman. When they married, she had been naive and innocent. For ten years, her husband had not given her the remotest hint that a woman is supposed to enjoy sex. Only recently, at the New School for Social Research, had she learned for the first time that a woman may have an orgasm. Through gnashing jaws, she spat out a furious ultimatum. It was her husband's duty to see to it that she had an orgasm or else!

An interesting phenomenon is the group of couples who swap partners for weekends. Many of these marriage deteriorate rapidly. In a few cases, however, there is a paradoxical response. The adventure of infidelity seems to have a remarkable healing effect on the marriage. It is a disturbing invasion of the lives of both partners, but strangely enough, if they pass through this crisis, each may emerge a stronger person. They experience mutual learning, and their companionship grows closer, their love life richer. They both grow as people. In one such case, the wife reacted to the shocking discovery of her husband's romance with an attractive Negro actress with the prompt disappearance of her sexual frigidity. This change delighted her husband and impelled him to characterize his Negro *amour* as the best psychotherapist he and his wife could have had.

This case is but one small example of the attitudes of the sex-seekers of our time. One way or another, they engage in a frantic search for new sexual kicks that they expect to be magic cure-alls.

In another case, a wife reacted with pathological jealousy. She was "bugged" on her husband's imagined sexual antics with other playmates; she plagued him incessantly. She was depressed, agitated, unable to sleep—nor did she let her husband sleep. She knew that her husband had erotic interests in women wrestlers and weight-lifters. When her husband asked her to lift him or hold him in her lap she refused. "It might break my back." She entered the role of detective in order "to get the goods" on her husband. She discovered in his desk a batch of pictures of female weight-lifters in scanty attire. Finding a stain on her husband's underclothing, she sent a piece of it to the chemical laboratory. The report came back: "positive; many spermatozoa were found together with large numbers of squamous epithelial cells. The finding of many squamous epithelial cells is indicative of the presence of vaginal secretion along with the spermatozoa." This evidence clinched the wife's case. She crucified her husband with this "proof." She demanded that he confess the truth. What new sexual tricks had he learned from "these other broads"?

Both partners had been previously married, so that in this household there were three sets of children, the wife's children by her former marriage, the husband's children by his former marriage, and a new baby. From the word "go" the partners failed completely to build a true marital union. The courtship phase was intense. Both parties moved fast to dissolve their previous marriages to make way for this one. But they were hardly married before the husband began to withdraw interest. When his wife became pregnant, he stopped making sexual advances altogether. Sensing his sexual rejection, she then began to develop jealous delusions.

In this case, husband and wife came from very different cultural and religious backgrounds, but they had in common the special experience of a philandering, unfaithful father. Each, however, reacted in a different way. The husband sided with his father. He felt convinced that his father had in fact been killed by his mother. Through her persistent nagging and accusations of infidelity, he believed she had caused his father's final heart collapse. The wife, on the other hand, entered in empathic alliance with her mother, in an attempt to protect the wounded pride of the females of the family against what she felt was her father's cold, ruthless, and indiscriminate indulgence in sexual escapades.

In therapy, the wife related four dreams in succession. In each, she depicted a threesome involved in a horrible tangle, reflecting the profound emotional connections between conflict in her marriage and older sources of conflict in her family of origin.

To illustrate, in one such dream, she found herself in an automobile, a convertible accompanied by her husband and his secretary, who was the object of her paranoid sexual jealousy. The three drove to the home of the patient's former husband, where she found other people. First, she spotted her father hiding in the bedroom, as if he were up to some mischief. Although he offered a plausible excuse for his presence, she knew that it was a complete lie. Then she became aware of the presence of other people—children, her husband's parents, his office secretary's parents, and so forth.

In this dream, we see three networks of family relationships, the husband's family, the wife's family, and the family of the secretary. We see the patient in the roles of both child and wife. At the very least, this dream reflects the complexity of the origins of marital jealousy in a way that embraces an extensive web of conflicted family relationships stretching across three generations. Marital disorders are clearly anything but simple. They are one aspect, a focal one to be sure, but nonetheless one aspect of an ongoing family phenomenon.

In our studies at The Family Mental Health Clinic in New York City, we have been oriented mainly toward these problems in the wider context of the family. We have preferred, at least in the first phase, to interview distressed marital partners together with their children and sometimes with their parents. The procedure is first to conduct a series of exploratory interviews with the whole family and then at the appropriate time to shift to specialization on the marital part of the broader family problem.

We learn to diagnose marital disorders by treating them. The marital relationship neither exists nor evolves in isolation. It has family in back of it; it has family ahead of it. Where there is marital conflict, it often involves prior conflicts between the respective partners and their families of origin. Marital conflict is often displaced and reprojected, in modified form, into the relations of each partner with the offspring. The original problems of each partner with the family of origin are thus projected across time into husband-wife and parent-child relations. The marital relationship does not and cannot stand still. It moves forward or backward. It grows, or it withers. It must be nourished, it must make way for change, it must respond to new experience—otherwise it dies. As the marital balance shifts from one stage of the family cycle to the next, the diagnostic judgment must change accordingly. The diagnosis of marital disorders is complicated. It is influenced by the ways in which the disorder is viewed from different places by different people with different interests and purposes: by the marital partners themselves; by other parts of the nuclear and extended families and community; by the professional worker. The range and diversity of marital disorders in our culture are enormous. Our interest is not only how the relationship works but also to what ends. Diagnosis can be approached at three levels: descriptive, genetic, and functional.

At the descriptive level, we can classify disorders of the marital partnership in terms of symptom clusters reflecting deviant patterns of interaction—for example, in sexual failure, economic or social failure, persistent quarreling, misunderstanding, alienation, and disturbances of communication, sharing, and identification.

At the dynamic level, diagnosis means the definition of the core conflicts, the ways of coping, the patterns of complementarity and failure of complementarity, the distortion and imbalance of the multiple functions of the marital interaction, and finally, the realism, maturity, stability, and growth potential of the relationship. From an estimate of these characteristics, we can delineate what is inappropriate and warped alongside what is appropriate and healthy in the quality of the marital adaptation.

At the genetic level, we trace the dynamic evolution of the relationship through the phases of courtship, early marriage, the arrival of the first child, and finally the expansion of the family with more children.

Diagnosis of marital interaction may be subdivided according to current performance, level of achievement, origin and development, and deviation measured against an ideal of a healthy marital relationship.

1. *Current Performance*
   a. capacity for love
   b. mutual adaptation, adaptation to external change, and adaptation for growth
   c. levels of benign conflict and destructive conflict; patterns of coping; interplay of shared defenses of the continuity of the marriage relationship with individual defenses against conflict and anxiety; and finally the characteristic patterns of complementarity (In clinical terms, two features of defense are of special importance: first, the use of the relationship and adaptation to the marital roles to compensate for anxiety in one or the other partner, to offer support against emotional break-

down, and second, the use of external relationships to mitigate failure in the marital relationship and to provide compensatory satisfactions of individual needs.)

    d. the quality of each partner's integration into his marital role and the fit of marital with other family roles

2. *Level of Achievement*
    a. the strivings, expectations, values, and needs of the relationship and of each partner
    b. the maturity, realism, and stability of the relationship
    c. the trends toward fixation, regression, disintegration, and so forth
    d. the discrepancy between actual performance and an ideal

3. *Origin and Development of the Relationship: From Courtship to the Time of Referral*
    a. influence of the evolving patterns of motivation, of the ideals and images of future marriage and family on the development of the marital partnership
    b. influence of the same factors (including children) on the development of the parental partnership
    c. areas of satisfaction, dissatisfaction, harmony and conflict, and healthy and unhealthy functioning
    d. past achievement in relation to values, expectations, and strivings

4. *Discrepancy Between the Actual Performance and an Ideal Model of Healthy Marital Functioning*

Disorders of the marital relationship are clinically expressed in two ways, as conflict over differences and failure of complementarity.

Conflict over differences becomes organized in a special way. Neither of the marital partners fights the battle alone. Each tends to form a protective alliance with other family members, children, grandparents, collateral relatives. In this way, the family splits into opposing factions. One partner engages in prejudicial scapegoating of the other. Each warring partner puts on blinders and attaches a menacing meaning to the difference. The inevitable result is a war of prejudice revolving around subjectively distorted representations of difference, rather than around actual ones. This war rests on the false belief that striving for one way of life automatically excludes another. Each faction then tries to impose its preferred set of aims and values on the relationship. The manifestations of this conflict appear as disturbances of empathy, union, and identification; as chronic destructive quarreling, often about wrong or trivial matters; as defects of communication; as the failure of devices for restoration of balance following upset; and finally in progressive alienation of the partners.

The outcome of such conflict depends less on the nature of the conflict than on the ways of coping with it. Coping with marital conflict is a shared function. It is carried on at both interpersonal and intrapersonal levels. In this connection, it is essential to trace the interplay between specific patterns for group defense of the continuity of the marriage relationship and individual defenses against the destructive effects of conflict and anxiety. At the relationship level, we may specify these patterns of defense: enhancement of the bond of love, sharing, co-operation, and identification; shifts in the complementarity of marital role adaptation brought about by a shared quest for the solution of conflicts, improved mutual need satisfaction, mutual support of self-esteem, support for the needed defenses against anxiety, and support of the growth of the relationship and of each partner as an individual; rigidification or loosening of the marital roles; reduction of conflict intensity by means of manipulation, coercion, bribery, compromise, compensation, denial, or escape; shifting alignments and splits within the family and prejudicial scapegoating of one part of the family by another, repeopling of the group, that is, the elimination of one member or the addition of another or a significant change in environment.

Failure in these patterns of coping produces, in turn, progressive failure of the quality of complementarity. The manifestations of such failure can be identified as particular units of interaction that become rigidified, automatized, inappropriate, and useless for the shared tasks of marital living.

The marital partnership may be oriented mainly to different goals, as in these examples:

1. A marital relationship in which each partner egocentrically preserves his premarital individuality largely untouched by the requirements of the marital bond.

2. A relationship in which the individuality of each partner is subordinated to the requirements of his marital role.
3. A relationship in which the individuality of each partner is subordinated to the requirements of his parental role.
4. A relationship in which the individuality of each partner is subordinated to conformity with the demands of the surrounding community.

Genetic or developmental failures include

1. The accidental or unintended marriage like, for example, a marriage necessitated by pregnancy.
2. The abortive or temporary marriage, begun as a kind of adventure, a trial marriage, or a conversion of a sexual affair and not basically intended to endure or to evolve into a family group.
3. The marriage used as a means to escape from conflict to rebel against the family of origin or to rebound from a prior disappointment in love.
4. The arranged marriage, which is a matter of security, of expediency, or of joining two larger families.

From the functional point of view, there are

1. The immature or protective marriage, motivated mainly by the need of one partner to relate, in the role of child, to the other in the role of parent.
2. The competitive marriage based on concealed envy, jealousy, and competitive admiration.
3. The marriage of neurotic complementarity, in which the special neurotic needs of one partner are complemented by those of the other, in which one partner serves as the healer of the conflicts and anxieties of the other. (The stronger partner in this arrangement is intended to serve as a provider of immunity against emotional breakdown in the more vulnerable partner.)
4. The marriage of complementary acting out, in which the two partners share an unconscious complicity in patterns of acting out conflicted urges.
5. The marriage of mutual emotional detachment, in which a tolerable balance is struck between the partners on the basis of a degree of emotional distance and isolation.
6. The master-slave marriage, a role partnership in which one partner seeks omnipotent control of the other. (Neither partner is a complete being. The master needs the slave; the slave needs the master. The one is aggrandized as the other is demeaned. The natural goals of love, sharing, and identification are perverted to the goal of power to dominate, degrade, and ultimately destroy

the partner. In essence, this bond is a symbiotic one, in which one partner expands at the expense of the other. A pathological balance of this type can be maintained only by means of co-ercion and intimidation.)

7. The regressive marriage dominated by a negative orientation to life. (There are shared fear of and prejudice against life and growth, shared expectation of imminent catastrophe. Implicit in the emotional content of such a partnership is the theme of total sacrifice. One partner must surrender the right to live and breathe in order to ensure the continued life of the other. In emotional orientation, the persons involved move backward in life, rather than forward. This type of marital couple is the most likely to produce psychotic offspring.)

8. The healthy marriage. (In this theoretical model or "pure" type, the partners have a good "fit" in the marital roles. They are able to share realistic goals and compatible values. When conflict arises, there may be transitory upset, yet, in the main, they are able to co-operate in the search for solution or appropriate com-promise. A temporary disturbance does not involve excessive or persistent accusation, guilt feelings, and scapegoating. Each part-ner has a genuine respect for and acceptance of the other as a person, a tolerance of differences, and, more than that, a willing-ness to use them for the creative growth of the relationship.)

To a large extent, diagnosis rests on the therapist's special interest—on what he is trying to do about the marital condition. In this context, diagnosis is no mere label but an integral aspect of a plan of action, a strategy for inducing change. Through the implementation of the principles and criteria described here, we seek a more precise definition of the functional pattern of the marital partnership, not only how it works but also to what ends. We want to know what it stands for, its goals and aspirations, what keeps the couple together, what pulls the partners apart. In essence, we seek to learn what is separate and what is shared in the relation-ship.

We turn now to the challenge of treatment. In keeping with the concepts we have outlined, the psychotherapy of marital disorders is viewed as the focused treatment of a component of family disorder. It is a phase of family therapy, adapted to and specialized for the specific features of a marital problem. Because family begins with marriage, the disorder of marital interaction is a focal point in family dynamics and development.

As I have discussed elsewhere my views of the method of family psychotherapy, I shall merely highlight here those special considerations pertaining to problems of marital interaction.

Professional contact begins with exploration of the salient problems, a function of any therapeutically oriented interview. In fact, we initiate the treatment process before we know what the problem is all about. Only as we become engaged in the adventure of therapy, do we achieve, step by step, a systematic diagnosis.

How is the marital trouble viewed? How do the partners see the problem, the family, and the community? What is the same and what is different in these several views? What alternatives loom up? What has the couple tried? What has it not tried? Or what has it tried in the wrong way? Do the partners feel discouraged, beaten down? Have they surrendered hope and given in to feelings of despair? Do they console themselves with mutual punishment? In any case, what do the partners now want? What does the family want of them? What does the community expect? What does each partner need of the other, of the family, and of the community? In turn, what is each partner willing to do for the other, for the family, and for the community? Finally, what is the orientation of the therapist? What does he, in his turn, propose to do?

These are the pertinent questions that confront the therapist at the outset. To make effective progress in clarifying the issues and exploring the alternatives, he must cultivate an optimal quality of contact, rapport, and communication between the marital partners and between them and himself. He uses this rapport to catalyze the main kinds of conflict and coping. He clarifies the real content of conflict by dissolving barriers, defensive disguises, confusions, and misunderstandings. By stages, he moves toward a more accurate mutual understanding with the marital partners of what is wrong. By stimulating empathy and communication, he seeks to arouse and enhance a live, honest, and meaningful emotional interchange. Figuratively speaking, he strives to make the contact a touching experience, a spontaneous and deeply genuine kind of communion. As the partners feel in touch with the therapist, they come into better touch with each other. Through the therapist's use of himself, his open, earnest sharing of his own emotions, he sets an example for the desired quality of interaction between the marital partners.

In the therapy of marital disorders, the therapist must know what he stands for, what he is trying to do. He must also know what he can and cannot do. He must have explicit awareness of his own ideology of marriage and family life. He must clearly define, in his own mind, whatever discrepancy prevails between his personal family values and those of the marital couple.

So often a central feature of marital conflict is competitiveness. Both partners are dedicated to the game of one-upmanship. Each seeks to get the best of the other. It is as if the business ethic of profit and loss invades the inner life of the married couple. Neither can be convinced of a gain unless he imposes a loss upon the partner, a semblance of sacrifice. The game of one-upmanship is the pursuit of a delusion. It is misleading, for it can end only in futility. The essence of the delusion is that the well-being of the one partner comes only with a measure of sacrifice and surrender from the other. In the marital relationship it cannot be that what is good for one is bad for the other. In the long view, what is good or bad for one must also be good or bad for the other. The very survival, continuity, and growth of marriage and family hinge on the acceptance of the principles of love, sharing, and co-operation. Without such acceptance, marriage and family have no meaning.

The goals of therapy for marital disorders are to alleviate emotional distress and disability and to promote the levels of well-being of both together and of each partner as an individual. In a general way, the therapist moves toward these goals by strengthening the shared resources for problem-solving; encouraging the substitution of more adequate controls and defenses for pathogenic ones; enhancing immunity against the disintegrative effects of emotional upset; enhancing the complementarity of the relationship; and promoting the growth of the relationship and of each partner as an individual.

The therapist is a participant-observer. To achieve the goals of marital therapy, the clinician must integrate his trained knowledge and his use of himself in the therapeutic role in a unique way. He must be active, open, flexible, forthright, at times even blunt. He must make the most free and undefensive use of himself. He moves alternately in and out of the pool of marital conflict. He moves in to energize and influence the interactional process; he moves out to distance himself, to survey and assess significant events, to objectify his experience, and then he moves in again. The marital partners engage in a selective process of joining with and separating from specific elements of the therapist's identity. The marital partners absorb, interact with, and use the therapist's influence in a variety of ways. The partial emotional joinings and separations reflect elements of transference and realism. The therapist must be adroit and constantly alert to shift his influence from one aspect of the marital relationship to another, following the shifting core of the most destructive conflict. He engages the partners in a progressive process of working through these conflicts. In the process, he fulfills multiple functions. He is catalyst, supporter, regulator, interpreter, and resynthesizer. These functions cannot be conceived in isolation but rather as a harmony of influences expressed through the unity of the therapist's use of himself.

He undercuts the tendency of the marital partners to console themselves by engaging in mutual blame and punishment. He stirs hope of a new and better relationship. He pierces misunderstandings, confusions, and distortions to reach a consensus with the partners about what is really wrong. In working through the conflicts over differences, the frustrations, defeats, and failure of complementarity, he shakes up the old deviant patterns of alignment and makes way for new avenues of interaction. He weighs and balances the healthy and sick emotional forces in the relationship. He supports the tendencies toward health and counteracts those toward sickness by shifting his function in accordance with need at changing stages of the treatment.

To sum up in more specific terms, once having established the needed quality of rapport, empathy, and communication and having reached a consensus about what is wrong, he moves ahead, implementing the following special techniques:

the counteraction of inappropriate denials, displacements, and rationalizations of conflict;

the transformation of dormant and concealed interpersonal conflict into open, interactional expression;

the lifting of hidden intrapersonal conflict to the level of interpersonal interaction;

the neutralization of patterns of prejudicial scapegoating that fortify the position of one marital partner while victimizing the other;

the penetration of resistances and the reduction of shared currents of conflict, guilt, and fear through the use of confrontation and interpretation;

the use of the therapist's self in the role of a real parent as a controller of interpersonal danger, a source of emotional support and satisfaction, a provider of emotional elements the marital couple needs but lacks (The last function is a kind of substitutive therapy in which the therapist feeds into the emotional life of the parties certain more appropriate attitudes, emotions, and images of marital and family relationships, which the couple has not previously had. By these means, the therapist improves the level of complementarity of the relationship.);

the therapist's use of himself as the instrument of reality testing;

the therapist's use of himself as educator and as personifier of useful models of health in marital interaction.

Using these various techniques, he proceeds, together with the marital couple, to test a series of alternative solutions to the marital distress.

10

CLINICAL ILLUSTRATIONS FROM PSYCHOANALYTIC FAMILY THERAPY

Martin Grotjahn

Doctor Grotjahn is well known as a provocative teacher, a deeply intuitive clinician, and a sophisticated experimentalist. He carries the torch of experimentation in psychotherapy that Franz Alexander carried before him, yet he works at all times within the psychoanalytic system. His book Psychoanalysis and the Family Neurosis *is another "must" for those interested in marital problems. His opinions are based on clinical analytic experience and "are stated with indifference to both conformity and controversy."*

In Defense of Some Psychoanalytic Concepts as a Basis for Family Treatment

In all the years of my practical work as a psychiatrist, psychoanalyst, and psychotherapist, I have been guided by therapeutic skepticism, which is almost traditional for a German psychiatric background. I consider psychoanalysis an essential part of training for almost any member of the healing profession. The psychoanalysis of a therapist is apt to protect patient and therapist against many errors in countertransference difficulties, which are the tool of our trade and its greatest danger.

Therapeutic skepticism has shown me that the therapeutic efficiency of psychoanalysis is limited; therapeutic psychoanalysis contrasts, to a certain extent, with psychoanalysis as an investigative method, which has not been used to the point of its limitations.

The use of psychoanalysis as an instrument of treatment is not a sacrosanct ritual, and we should feel free to change

it as our analytic insights into the dynamics of the therapeutic process deepen. More and more of the same is not
enough: If an analysis of 300 hours has not shown the
desired results, it is not certain that an analysis ten times
as long will finally yield success. Contemporary psychoanalysis tends to last longer and longer, which may at times
be therapeutically necessary and unavoidable. Clinical
experience has shown that duration is not necessarily, however, a sign of depth, thoroughness, or efficiency.

The future of psychoanalysis does not seem to lie in
unaltered technique. Combinations of all kinds of action
and interaction with pharmacology and group approaches
will have to be tried, and Sigmund Freud himself would
approve of this experimentation—for he predicted and
hoped for many changes in this science of which he laid the
foundations in his pioneering work.

Psychoanalytic family therapy implies a dynamic approach and a genetic understanding of the family. Such
understanding must include the conscious and the unconscious of all the individuals involved, their personalities,
their neuroses, their interactions. It must go even further:
It must also include—with special emphasis—the complementary neuroses, the normal and the abnormal interactions
among the family members themselves and with the family
therapist.

This kind of family therapy is correctly called "analytic"
because it takes into careful consideration the transference
situation, which, in everyday family therapy, is so often
overlooked in favor of interaction. It also takes into careful
consideration resistance—even though a family's resistance
can be expected to differ somewhat from individual character resistance as we know it from psychoanalysis.

This approach to family therapy is explicitly analytic
because the basis of therapeutic intervention is the interpretation of the unconscious and of the patient's resistance
to having it made conscious. Such interpretation aims at
insight and integration. All such insight must be part of
emotional experience. Psychoanalytic family therapy is an

intensive, deep experience, and this fact—together with some specific features in the process of working through—makes family treatment so often effective.

Sigmund Freud himself was a representative of what could be called a "negative family therapy." In "Recommendations for Physicians in the Analytic Method" (1912), he wrote, "When it comes to the treatment of relatives, I must confess myself utterly at a loss and I have altogether little faith in any individual therapy of them."

Later (in his "General Introduction to Psychoanalysis"), Freud wrote, "Because when the husband's resistance is added to that of the sick wife, efforts are made fruitless and therapy is prematurely broken off." He added, "We had undertaken something which under existing conditions was impossible to carry out." Nevertheless, Freud knew the dynamics of the family neurosis, which he described for the first time in his paper, "The Family Romance." He was also aware of unconscious communication ("The Unconscious," 1915): "It is remarkable that the unconscious of one human being can react upon that of another without the conscious being implicated at all."

A Short Note on Unconscious Communication

This clinical essay is not the place to go into the details and theories of unconscious communication. Perhaps it is more fitting to report briefly a case history that may illustrate a bizarre communication between two men struggling to solve their respective conflicts about latent homosexuality, with corresponding death fears and murderous wishes.

The man who came to me for help was a lawyer who was being persecuted by a former client of his, who had some reason to feel injured, as the lawyer had had a brief affair with the client's wife. There was some evidence that the client—unconsciously—had arranged the seduction of his wife by the lawyer, who then reacted with great guilt and fear. The lawyer was afraid of being murdered by the en-

raged husband; his disproportionate fear was especially sur-
prising as he had given astonishing evidence of his almost
superhuman courage in the war, during which he had been
decorated for bravery several times.

During the interviews, it developed that this great war
hero had all his life fought his fear of being a coward and
of dying. The analyst's interpretation that the fear of dying
is often a disguised wish to kill found unexpected confirma-
tion in the lawyer's associations following the interpretation: His father had deserted him before his birth and
had left him in the care of a powerful, domineering mother.
The lawyer developed an intense hatred for his father,
which once culminated in a terrible fight, during which the
city's police had to be summoned to separate the embattled
father and son.

Unconsciously, this man had seduced his paranoid-schizo-
phrenic client into re-enacting the unresolved homosexual
love-hate relationship with his father. These two men
engaged in a truly murderous duel on the outskirts of the
town where they lived—yet called each other by their first
names. The fight ended in a draw, for both men were well
trained commandos with extensive combat experience. The
lawyer tried to settle his struggle with himself, his homosexuality, his longing for love, and his simultaneous need
to express his hatred for his father by projecting these intolerable feelings upon his persecutor. He wanted to experience the murder passively, for he felt too guilty actively to
murder his father or the father's symbolic representative.
The whole scene was not re-enacted on genital or oedipal
levels: That would have been less dangerous and not so near
to a psychotic danger point. The combat was a re-enactment
on much deeper, cannibalistic levels. The paranoid-schizo-
phrenic partner represented not only the absent father but
also the living, domineering, devouring, phallic mother—
from whom the lawyer had never succeeded in liberating
himself.

Insight and guidance, based on analytic insight into the

dynamics of this arrangement and into the unconscious communication between these two men, helped the lawyer to resolve his projection, even though' it was not possible to resolve his deeper, underlying conflicts. In this way, by withdrawing the projections from the client, great and very real danger could be eliminated and tragic consequences avoided. It became obvious to me that further treatment probably would lead to a paranoid, extremely hostile, and regressive transference psychosis. It therefore seemed advisable to interrupt treatment after six interviews.

Five years of follow-up study have shown that this man has achieved some kind of adjustment, which appears on the surface to be adequate.

Diagnostic Family Interviews

It is my experience that brief, diagnostic interviews with families may reveal family dynamics in ways that are more dramatic and convincing than those of any other conceivable method of teaching psychodynamic reasoning. Much can be learned from a well conducted interview with an individual patient, from his productions, his free-associative anamnesis, perhaps from a few dreams. And we can gain additional clues and hints from his motoric behavior in the interview situation and his relationship with the therapist. But our interpretation is to a large extent a matter of applied experience, of preconceived concepts and well confirmed conclusions, which make the patient and his unconscious understandable. During a family interview, the unconscious dynamics of such a group of people become evident before our eyes we must only be able to see it. We actually see the relationship and interaction between a mother and her child; we see them interacting, getting involved or not involved; we see the relationship, perhaps the alliance, between father and mother, their relationships with the children, interaction between siblings, the transference of the family's past to the present therapeutic situation with the therapist. The learning experience becomes three-dimensional.

A colleague introduced me to a family of which one daughter had been committed to the clinic first because of a psychotic episode the previous night.

It was already revealing to see how the family moved into the examination room and how the members seated themselves. The father, fifty-eight years old and a powerful figure, entered the consultation room first. He seemed uncomfortable in his Sunday best; he was being maneuvered from behind by his wife, aged fifty-nine, who was seated behind him, half-hidden, looking bitter, anxious, and guilty. Behind the mother, also half-hidden, was the oldest daughter, thirty-two years old, seated like a puppeteer, controlling the strings to her parents with her right hand, while her left hand held two invisible strings to her two younger sisters, seated on her left. The middle daughter, aged twenty-five, behaved and spoke like a beatnik. She was sitting very close and actually in physical contact with the last member of the family, the "baby," who was nineteen but actually appeared about twelve. This youngest daughter was the hospitalized psychotic patient.

Within forty-five minutes, it became clear to everyone—including the least sophisticated student or the most resistant observer of this family in interaction—that the three daughters represented three different degrees of maternal rejection: The father, a truck driver, worked at night and slept during the day. He had become a heavy drinker. The eldest and most mature daughter had been conceived and reared during the period of parental bliss. Seven years later, a second daughter was conceived with indifference during a drunken rape. She had grown up a beatnik, living periodically away from home, engaging in promiscuous affairs. Finally, the baby was conceived, unexpected, unwanted, actively hated, and the victim of death wishes from the mother. Further complicating her existence was her reaction to the religiosity of this family and to the guilt of the psycho-

pathic middle daughter, who seemed to relate herself to the
"baby" by saying, "I am a beatnik; I am the promiscuous
one. You are the nun; you take the veil." In her psychotic
episode, the "baby" tried to combine her need to seek
acceptance in the church with her need to participate in her
sister's sexual sins by running out of the house at two o'clock
in the morning undressed and seeking her priest for con-
fession.

No insight into the patient alone could have been so
deep, so revealing, so clear and convincing, so three-dimensional as that provided by witnessing this schizophrenic girl
reacting, so to speak, on the stage of the family theater, in
her relationships with her parents, sisters, and herself.

Such diagnostic dynamic family consultations are an
invaluable teaching aid to the dynamically oriented therapist. My experience has also shown me that such brief diagnostic interviews have some intrinsic therapeutic effects:
The members of the family look at one another—so to speak
—with the eyes of the therapist. They do not see one another
so clearly as does the therapist, but definitely differently
from the way they formerly did.

A Brief Illustration of Psychoanalytic Family Therapy

It is not possible within the framework of this report on
practical experience from psychoanalytic family therapy to
give an accurate account of the course of one such family
under treatment. Only a specimen situation can be given,
which is regrettable, for less illustrative material can be
shown. This family has been under treatment and observation for four years.

The specimen situation selected stresses one peculiar
aspect of psychoanalytic family therapy: that working
through is different in this setting from that of psychoanalysis or even from group psychotherapy. The working
through in psychoanalysis starts in a one-to-one relationship,

is then internalized, and continues within the patient out-side the analyst's office. In group psychotherapy, the process of working through is slightly different: Insight is gained, tried, and tested through group interaction. After the end of the group session, the process of working through is in-terrupted, perhaps stopped or internalized, approximately as in individual psychoanalysis. After the group session, each member becomes again an individual patient, trying to deal with himself.

The family group reacts quite differently, and this signifi-cant difference has not been sufficiently considered in psycho-analytic literature. The process of working through the family conflict (or the family constellation) is neither inter-rupted nor ended nor necessarily even internalized. It continues as if in a group that meets in uninterrupted session for weeks and months of life and growth, of sickness and maturation, and of constant interpretation of existence together (special utilization of this aspect of family therapy has led to the technique of m.i.t., multiple impact therapy, as developed by the Galveston team of psychotherapists). It is this aspect that is illustrated in our specimen situation.

The father was a suspicious, intensely hostile man of forty-five. He came of German stock and was authoritarian, rigid, seemingly unloving, righteous—to the point of bru-tality—not given to use any of his wealth. He was the oldest of a gang of brothers, but he had left the gang early to attend boarding school far away from home. Each time he came home on vacation, his mother was pregnant again, and he had to leave soon again in order to make room for a newly arrived brother. Once, while the patient was attend-ing his commanding post at harvest time, a younger brother was caught by a monstrous harvesting machine, leaving the patient with the sign of Cain and a life-long depressive guilt.

His wife, only a year her husband's junior, had married him during the war. She came from an enormous family whose members all lived together, forming practically a little town. She had one older brother and one younger brother: a combination that sometimes produces the almost perfect woman who has learned from her older brother how to obey and from her younger brother how to care for little boys and make men of them.

The couple had six children: four girls and two boys, ranging in ages from twenty-two to ten years. The youngest, however, looked only half her age, demonstrating the psychosomatic influence of a strong family trend to keep the baby just that.

In the first year of conjoint therapy, nothing was accomplished: I was discouraged from the start, appalled by the rigidity of the husband but impressed by the strength and the despair of his wife. Previous therapists had advised the woman to take her children and leave her husband—and possibly the state.

My interpretation of the situation at that time could be summarized: "He wants you to liberate him from his family. He will hate you if you should try that. He loves his mother, and he hates her. He loves her because he never felt loved by her—but still hopes for it. He hates her because he feels it was she who made him leave the house when one after the other of his brothers was born. Now, in his marriage, he is trying to split his emotions by loving his mother and hating you, his wife. He will always try to punish you because he will make you responsible for what he considers to be his mother's sins. No psychiatrist can help much—perhaps only you can."

I also saw some motives in the woman for not following the psychiatrists' advice to leave her husband. While he fought her, she, in an antiparanoid attitude, had to fight for him—as she had learned to fight for love in her enormous family.

In my attitude toward both, I played the role of the innocent bystander.

After this first year of consulting, observing, waiting, and cautious interpreting, the wife wrote a letter that revealed her warmth and her maturity, her gift for understanding her family, and also her ability to express herself—

even when crying in despair for help. She wanted to be seen, and she wanted to be seen with all her children. I invited them all to come after office hours, so that we should not have to worry about keeping another patient waiting.

These family interviews in the late afternoon became a kind of family feast: There was a long (one to one and one-half hours) drive, which began shortly after lunch; then, upon arriving in my neighborhood, the family scattered for window-shopping, perhaps a movie, some reading in the car, or even studying, and, naturally, there was some eating. Finally, around five, the whole troup united in my waiting room. In this contact among the different family members, the coming interview was freely discussed, and the atmospheric conditions were prepared.

The father was always invited but never appeared. I interpreted his behavior as that of an oldest son who had had to leave his family and who had now succeeded in forcing his new family to leave him.

As a rule, the proceedings started with the mother's complaint: "All the children are against me. They all say that I feed them garbage, which is exactly what their father says. They tell me I buy cheap stuff, whereas I have to economize. They complain that I am always busy." I said nothing but observed the mother's paranoid reaction to her husband's hostility.

The children would complain about their unfulfilled needs for a father and about their guilt. These complaints would lead to their mother's complaint that the children always wanted to have "peace at any price," that they could not stand to witness fighting or bickering between the parents, but she could not always submit. She had to defend herself and her children against their father's tyranny and brutality. None of these problems was solved, but all were stated.

At times, the attention of the entire group was focused on the "baby," and it was the opinion of all that she was most in danger. One of the two brothers explained that he also had been most unhappy when he had occupied the room in which the baby now slept, which was closest to the parental bedroom. It was quite clear at that moment that everybody was talking about the fighting between the parents but was simultaneously concerned about some primal-scene observation. I employed the technique of "silence pregnant with meaning." I did not think sexual matters between the generations should be discussed at this time in the mother's presence—especially when it became so obvious what was in everybody's mind. Later, the older girls turned against their brothers, by whom they felt rejected or at least not accepted. After this problem was discussed, it turned out that both boys and girls got along fairly well, especially when out on dates with other boys and girls. The oldest daughter volunteered to tell a *dream,* in which she saw a girl being persecuted, running away, then brought back in handcuffs by two men—probably representing her two brothers. Here again, for the time being, no interpretation was offered, but later associations demonstrated how much the girl in the dream enjoyed the fact that she was handcuffed.

From there, her associations went to a favorite family game in which again the sexual connotations were obvious. Finally, one of the boys presented a *dream,* in which he was a cowboy attacked by cows.

Here I gave an interpretation by inference. I said that I have often thought about the unconscious meaning of the cowboy story and have always noticed that the cowboy never gets the girl, but he does get the horse. After presentation of this dream, I realized that there might not be much difference. A little later, the children told me about their "horsing around," and the sexual undercurrent was clear to everyone and silently accepted. There was no need for permission, prohibition, or interpretation. Still, it was of great importance to bring this question into the open.

The second oldest girl then reported about her boyfriend. It was amazing to watch the understanding, the insight, and the natural tendency to growth and maturation within the family. Everyone saw quite clearly that this girl had chosen this boy as her friend because he was so much like her father. She wanted to cure this paranoid young man and do better than her mother had done with the paranoid father.

The transference situation of this family in treatment developed as it seemed to have found a kind, tolerant, understanding, patient, listening father, who was there to accept it and to try to understand it and to help its members understand one another. It resembled the transfer of a hope for a father into the reality of treatment more than the transfer of the past to the present.

After the sessions with me, the family usually started on the long drive home, which took approximately two hours and was interrupted for dinner. During this time, the entire family would continue the family session. Anyone who had felt left out had his or her chance. Topics were repeated and further worked through; new associations and material would be added, and opinions compared, changed, and elaborated. There were action, reaction, and interaction— and a fair amount of interpretation by whoever felt inspired to venture explanation.

As a rule, the mother found time to summarize the events between sessions in long letters—all excellently written, often containing dream material, and well suited to a study of family dynamics, their progress and regress, growth, maturation, and sickness. The father participated in some of these discussions and in a curious way became the therapist's counterpart—being involved without losing face by joining the treatment situation himself. He did not see me as an enemy; he related himself to me more as one sovereign to the chief of a neighboring tribe, to whom he has sent him family for a visit.

In the last (fourth) year of observation, when we had no more formal conferences, the slow fragmentation of the family could be observed. The two boys went away to college, as did some of the girls. Even "the baby," the youngest daughter, spent much of her time away from home with a neighboring family, who had three children younger than she. There she experienced a role reversal and found herself promoted from the family baby to "mother" of three.

The most remarkable progress was made by the always-absent father, in the form of delayed maturation. The mother had ample opportunity to satisfy her need to combat paranoia wherever she could find it: in her husband, in the community, in the school, and also in her periodical visits to her own large family of origin. She continued to write to me after she had moved from this area, and she continued a certain amount of working through in her letters. She found by herself an "open-end technique" for terminating family therapy.

No psychiatrist or family therapist could have been more effective than this brave woman in her difficult situation.

Conjoint Interviews as an Aid in Psychoanalysis

In my book *Psychoanalysis and the Family Neurosis*[1] I have described in detail the dynamics, the meanings, the techniques and the effects of conjoint interviews as a method to activate the therapeutic process in psychoanalysis and to increase its efficiency.[2] I have seen my patient's partner either alone or together with my patient in analysis; I have seen them only once or occasionally, frequently, regularly, or not at all when that was indicated. I have started additional therapy, or I have not; I have employed the interviews as a parameter of psychoanalytic technique in the early stages of psychoanalysis, during the course of psychoanalysis, during the terminal phase, or even after years of interrupted treatment. If my patient's partner is in analysis with a colleague, I gladly see the colleague too if he wishes to join us. I have also learned that a conference of two colleagues working with the same family may benefit from a conjoint conference with me—either with or without the patients. Such consultations may help to avoid unnecessary countertransference battles, which always take place on the backs of the patients. It sounds paradoxical, but it has been my experience nevertheless that, almost without fail, both analysts are justified in their complaints about the partners of their respective analysands. It is the beauty and the despair of work in our field that all embattled partners may be right but that they may never meet on the same level of communication in order to work out their difficulties. As long as they try to communicate on different levels of a multilayered, complex system of communication, they need a therapist to guide them to successful "in-fighting," as it were. In order to re-establish successful communication, the therapist must give insights into the multileveled nature of communications between human beings.

I start working with the expectations of my patients when I suggest a conjoint meeting. I work equally well with the acceptance of my suggestion, as I can deal with resistance against it. All this activity is to establish communication within a marriage both inside and outside the analysis. My main goal has always been and still is to gain insights into the unconscious meaning of my patient, his partner, and the complexity of the communication between them.

A part of such insights is the acknowledgment and discipline of my countertransference. Because my empathy and understanding make of my countertransference an essential therapeutic tool, I do not think that countertransference is a sign of insufficient self-analysis or insufficient discipline of the therapist. There is a great—and for me, obvious—difference between the use of countertransference in therapy and its abuse. The first calls for constant watching to gain new insights, the second calls for continuous analysis of the therapist.

I have described one such situation in *Psychoanalysis and the Family Neurosis*. A patient turned to his (male) analyst in depressive despair and developed a strong, positive mother transference to him, while at home his wife, in slowly deepening anguish, suffered nightmarish pain when the patient, in a split transference, treated her as if she were his bad mother. The analyst refused to recognize the wife's justifiable insistence to be seen and did not understand his patient's split transference emotion.

I have often emphasized—and have as often been misunderstood and criticized—that an analyst caught in such a situation who turns from his patient to the patient's marriage partner is not acting as a justice of the peace to investigate the truth or reality or the distribution of fault and guilt in a marriage. The family interviews give insight into the *dynamics* of such an unhappy marriage and such a complicated transference-countertransference situation. It is not true that such interviews complicate matters further. Our patients show us the way if we understand their clues and the messages they communicate to us.

Insight into unconscious arrangements as resistance to treatment is the object of such family interviews within the course of psychoanalysis. Understanding of the family dynamics and not investigation into the distribution of guilt is the aim—as we shall see. Here is an illustration from recent practice:

A skillful, experienced, and highly respected analyst sent me the wife of a patient of his, whom he had had in analysis for more than a year. This woman had been diagnosed by several psychiatrists as very sick, and I was supposed to see her in consultation and to refer her to proper hands. The referring analyst included in his letter this ominous sentence: "I see her, *of course*, only through the eyes of my patient." My immediate reaction was, Why does he see this woman through the eyes of his patient? And why "of course"? Even if the patient is very passive, dependent, demanding, infantile—he should nevertheless be able to tolerate the contact between his wife and his analyst, who should form his own personal impression of his patient's marriage partner. In my experience, no patient is too sick to tolerate this meeting. If, in the analyst's opinion, such a meeting cannot take place, then the resistance is likely *his* and not the patient's, and this point should be clear. Because in this case I happened to know both the analyst and the patient, I arrived at the thought that the patient's wish to be his analyst's only child was not exclusively his wish—that it was also the analyst's wish to fulfill his demands to a certain extent.

The husband accompanied his wife to my office. He was anxious and eager for me to see "how sick" his wife really was—which I promptly failed to see. His behavior clarified for me why his wife had been diagnosed as such a sick woman by my colleagues who had seen this woman previously.

To me, the woman's complaints were within the limits of understandable reaction: She complained about her absent husband, the horrible fights they had, and, most of all, she repeatedly complained, "His psychoanalyst does not know what goes on."

This woman came from a family with an older sister and an older brother and a younger sister and a younger brother. As a middle child, she had early learned how to work for her love and had succeeded. She also had the feeling that she never received the love she deserved. She carried this attitude over into her marriage. She worked hard—extremely hard—for the love of her husband and her children but received very little.

The husband had one older sister and one younger brother—he too was a middle child. His situation was further complicated, however, by the frequent hospitalization of his father for a schizophrenic psychosis.

My recommendation was further analysis for the man and occasional interviews for his wife. I explained that, due to the patient's personality, he had developed a split transference, in which he conveniently declared his analyst to be the good and all-knowing mother (who also substituted for the father he had never had), while to his wife he assigned the role of the bad, frustrating mother. As this split transference established a precarious balance, the conflict was never taken up in his analysis. In this situation, an occasional check-up with the partner of the patient in analysis is a medical necessity.

NOTES

1. Martin Grotjahn, *Psychoanalysis and the Family Neurosis* (New York: W. W. Norton and Company, Inc., 1960).
2. My general attitude toward psychoanalysis was formulated in my book, *Beyond Laughter* (Englewood Cliffs, N.J.: McGraw-Hill Book Co., Inc., 1957), and I described my approach to psychoanalytic family therapy in *Psychoanalysis and the Family Neurosis*. A detailed bibliography may be found there. Two forthcoming books apply my analytic thinking to other aspects of the vast analytic field: *Psychoanalytic Pioneers*, co-edited with Franz Alexander and Samuel Eisenstein (New York: Basic Books, Inc., 1965); and *The Symbol in Civilization: A Collection of Essays on Psychoanalysis,* to be published in 1965.

INDEX